Plant-Based Cookbook for Beginners 2023

The Complete Book of Tasty and Easy High-Protein Plant-Based Recipes for Everyday Meals | 40-Day Eating Plan Included for a Healthier Lifestyle

By

Colton Pearson

Table of Content

Introduction 8

Chapter 1: The Beginner's Guide 10

   1.1   The Five Groups Of Food 10

   1.2   Benefits 10

   1.3   How To Change To A Diet Based On Vegetables? 11

Chapter 2: The 40-Day Meal Plan 13

Chapter 3: Breakfast Recipes 19

   1.   Scrambled Avocado And Tofu Sandwich 19

   2.   Chia Strawberry Parfait 20

   3.   Mixed Berry Bowl 21

   4.   Mexican Hot Chocolate 21

   5.   Oatmeal With Figs And Banana 22

   6.   Breakfast Potatoes 23

   7.   Nutty Granola Alongside Dried Currants 24

   8.   Fruit Salad With Ginger-Lemon Syrup 25

   9.   Granola 25

   10.   Banana Fluffy Pancakes 26

   11.   Fry-Bread With Jam And Peanut Butter 27

   12.   Banana Blueberry Smoothie 28

   13.   Classic French Toast 28

   14.   Ciabatta Bread Pudding With Sultanas 29

   15.   Cherry Chocolate Smoothie 30

   16.   Tasty Oatmeal Muffins 31

   17.   Vegan Banh Mi 32

   18.   Omelet With Chickpea Flour 33

   19.   Nutty Oatmeal Morning Muffins 34

   20.   White Sandwich Bread 35

   21.   Chia And Raspberry Smoothie Bowl 37

   22.   A Toast To Remember 37

   23.   Morning Oats With Currants And Walnuts 38

   24.   Tasty Panini 39

25. Classic Applesauce Pancakes And Coconut 40

26. Mushroom And Onion Tart 41

27. Banana-Cinnamon French Toast 42

28. Indian Traditional Roti 43

29. Chia Chocolate Pudding 44

30. Easy Morning Polenta 45

31. Pepper And Scallion Omelet 45

32. Classic Tofu Scramble 46

Chapter 4: Beans And Grains Recipes **48**

1. Black Bean And Bulgur Chili 48

2. Red Kidney Bean Pâté 49

3. Ribollita Or Traditional Tuscan Bean Stew 50

4. Red Kidney Bean Salad 51

5. Anasazi Bean Stew 52

6. Soybean Chinese-Style Salad 53

7. Basic Amaranth Porridge 53

8. Quinoa Porridge With Dried Figs 54

9. Millet Porridge With Sultanas 55

10. Everyday Savory Grits 56

11. Rye Porridge With Blueberry Topping 56

12. Coconut Sorghum Porridge 57

13. Sweet Maize Easy Meal Porridge 57

14. Mom's Millet Muffins 58

15. Cornmeal Porridge With Maple Syrup 59

Chapter 5: Main Meals **61**

1. Tofu Teriyaki Stir-Fry 61

2. Avocado Toast With Chickpeas 62

3. Portobello Burger & Veggie Fries 63

4. Teriyaki Eggplant 65

5. Cauliflower Steak Kicking Corn 66

6. Mushroom Tomato Spaghetti Squash 67

7. Thai Seitan Vegetable Curry 68

8. Chipotle Roasted Chickpeas 69

9.   *Garlic Lime Roasted Asparagus* *69*

10.   *Piquillo Salsa Verde Steak* *70*

11.   *Smoked Tempeh & Broccoli Fritters* *71*

12.   *Vegan Chicken & Rice* *73*

13.   *Lemon Couscous & Tempeh Kabobs* *74*

14.   *Fresco Sofritas Tacos* *76*

15.   *Roasted Cheesy Asparagus* *77*

16.   *Noodles Alfredo With Herby Tofu* *78*

17.   *Cheesy Potato Casserole* *79*

18.   *Eggplant Stacks* *80*

19.   *Mushroom Marinated Wraps* *80*

20.   *Scalloped Potatoes* *81*

21.   *Green Onion And Mushroom Stir-Fry* *82*

22.   *Chickpeas And Rice* *83*

23.   *Spinach Casserole* *84*

24.   *Lime Pasta* *85*

25.   *Zucchini Meatballs* *86*

26.   *The Tempeh Chili* *87*

27.   *Mushroom Patties And Herbs* *88*

28.   *Stuffed Peppers* *89*

Chapter 6: Smoothies & Drinks **90**

1.   *Banana And Spinach Smoothie* *90*

2.   *Fruity Smoothie* *90*

3.   *Mango Smoothie* *91*

4.   *Spiced Warm Lemon Drink* *91*

5.   *Warm Pomegranate Punch* *92*

6.   *Nice Spiced Cherry Cider* *93*

7.   *Energizing Detox Ginger Tonic* *93*

8.   *Ultimate Mulled Wine* *94*

9.   *Soothing Tea Drink* *95*

10.   *Pleasant Lemonade* *95*

11.   *Fragrant Spiced Coffee* *96*

12.   *Rich Truffle Hot Chocolate* *97*

Chapter 7: Snacks & Desserts **98**

1. *Asparagus And Chickpeas Salad* 98

2. *Nori Snack Rolls* 99

3. *Avocado Toast With Flaxseeds* 100

4. *Cinnamon Oranges* 100

5. *Plant-Based Crispy Falafel* 101

6. *Spinach And Strawberry Salad* 102

7. *Fried Avocados* 103

8. *Apple Cinnamon Skillet* 103

9. *Baked Potato* 104

10. *Whole Wheat Chocolate Waffle* 104

11. *Balsamic Avocado* 105

12. *Strawberry Blender Pancakes* 106

13. *Orange Parfait* 107

14. *Caramelize Oven-Baked Plantains* 107

15. *Sweet Truffles* 108

16. *Carrot Fritters* 109

Chapter 8: Soups & Stews **111**

1. *Green Onion Soup* 111

2. *Roasted Creamy Beet Soup* 112

3. *Winter Bean Soup* 113

4. *Cucumber And Avocado Soup* 114

5. *Potato Soup* 114

6. *Amaranth Vegetable Soup* 115

7. *Chickpea, Acorn Squash, And Couscous Soup* 116

8. *Creamy Rutabaga Soup* 118

9. *Mexican-Style Chili Soup* 119

10. *Potato Creamed Soup With Herbs* 120

11. *Autumn Squash Soup* 121

12. *Grandma's Creamy Soup* 123

13. *Greek-Style Tomato And Pinto Bean Soup* 124

14. *Winter Root Vegetable Soup* 125

15. *Golden Creamy Veggie Soup* 126

16. *Cannellini Bean Soup And Kale* 128

17.   *Old-Fashioned Vegetable And Lentil Stew* 129

18.   *Green Lentil Stew And Collard Greens* 129

19.   *Cream Of Carrot Soup* 130

20.   *Bean Plus Vegetable Stew* 131

Chapter 9: Everyday Staples: Sauces, Spreads & Salad Dressings **133**

1.   *Classic Barbecue Sauce* 133

2.   *Walnut Ligurian Sauce* 133

3.   *Lime, Cashew, And Dill Sauce* 134

4.   *Cilantro Garlic Dressing* 135

5.   *Avocado Herb Salad Dressing* 135

6.   *Classic Ranch Dressing* 136

7.   *Homemade Guacamole* 137

8.   *French Authentic Remoulade* 137

9.   *Traditional Russian Chrain* 138

10.   *Country-Style Mustard* 139

Conclusion **140**

Introduction

A plant-based diet eliminates all animal products, including red meat, chicken, eggs, fish, and dairy goods and includes all whole grains, minimally processed fruits, vegetables, legumes, seeds and nuts, spices, and herbs.

Plant-forward or mostly plant-based eating emphasizes foods made from plants. It includes beans, legumes, whole grains, nuts, oils, vegetables, and seeds. While, it doesn't suggest that you are a vegan or vegetarian who avoids all animal products. Rather, a larger portion of your diet comprises meals from plant sources.

Vegetarian and Mediterranean diets

What is the proof that eating habits based on plants are beneficial?

Numerous studies on nutrition have looked at vegetarian and Mediterranean diets and other plant-based eating regimens. The mainstay of the Mediterranean diet is plant-based, with occasional additions of fish, eggs, chicken, yogurt, cheese, sweets, and meats.

The Mediterranean diet has been linked to a lower risk of metabolic syndrome, heart disease, diabetes, certain cancers, specifically breast, colon, and prostate cancer, depression, a lower risk of frailty in older adults, and improved physical and mental health in both large population studies and randomized clinical trials.

Additionally, vegetarian diets have been demonstrated to enhance health, including a reduced chance of acquiring diabetes, high blood pressure, and other cardiovascular diseases.

In addition to being richer in fiber and phytonutrients, plant-based diets include all the protein, lipids, carbs, minerals, and vitamins required for good health. To ensure they get all the nutrients they need, some vegans, particularly those who are vegan, might have to add a supplement, particularly vitamin B12.

If you wish to alter your eating habits, you must first determine why you'd like to do so. Does this result from peer pressure? Is it a result of your surroundings or health-related issues? Knowing your objective will make it simpler for you to stay with it. If this seems to be a big lifestyle adjustment, you must also prepare for some challenging future moments. Recognize that you may experience some withdrawal symptoms during the first several days. You're going to feel inclined to resume your old eating patterns. However, you could be able to restrain your impulses if you continuously recall yourself of your objectives.

Last, you must embrace this fresh phase in your life by having a positive and open perspective. Keep your attention on all the advantages that eating a plant-based diet will provide you. You may also outline these advantages from the diet and pin them up in your kitchen. You can keep on course by doing this. Starting and sticking with this new diet shouldn't require much willpower or effort. It should be about tasting new tastes, learning about new fresh spices, herbs, and plants and anything else intriguing. Don't make the trip about a battle, even if it could be challenging. A plant-based diet is more likely to become your new lifestyle choice if you like it, which increases your likelihood of sticking with it.

Chapter 1: The Beginner's Guide

You intend to adopt a plant-based diet, then. Maybe you'd like to eat less meat because you've heard it has health advantages, you care about the atmosphere, or you want to. You are not alone, whatever your motivations. Plant-based goods have recently flooded grocery shelves and are selling like hotcakes. Additionally, one in four Americans consume less meat, and sales of dairy products are declining.

So What Is a Plant-Based Diet?

Is the diet vegan? Vegetarian? Almost mostly plant-based, with occasional meat.

For others, it entails adhering to a strict vegan diet. Others interpret a plant-based diet as consisting mostly of vegetables with sporadic servings of dairy, meat, eggs, and fish. But the fundamental principles remain the same: consuming fewer animal products and eating more complete plant foods like fruit, whole grains, vegetables, nuts, legumes, and seeds.

1.1   The Five Groups of Food

An overview of the main food groups you'll find enjoyable on the plant-based diet is provided here for a more thorough explanation of what to eat while following a plant-based diet.

Vegetables: A variety of vegetables, such as peppers, lettuce, corn, spinach, peas, kale, collard greens, etc., are available.

Whole grains: It includes unprocessed cereals, grains, and other starches, including brown rice, quinoa, oats, popcorn, oats, etc.

Fruits: Any fruit, such as citrus fruits, apples, grapes, bananas, and strawberries.

Tubers: Yucca, yams, sweet potatoes, and other starchy root crops are examples of tubers.

Legumes: These include all types of beans, lentils, pulses, etc.

You may also eat other foods, such as whole-grain pieces of bread and flour, tofu, nuts, tempeh, avocados, seeds, and plant-based milk. However, since they are higher in calories and may lead to weight gain, we advise consuming these meals in moderation.

1.2   Benefits

Increasing your diet of plant-based foods provides several long-term health advantages for your body. Some individuals adopt a plant-based diet because it may help them lose weight, improve their health, and create tasty meals with extra nutritional advantages.

A plant-based diet is appropriate for a variety of reasons, such as:

1. Fiber Intake Boost

Like avocados, many vegetables and fruits are rich in fiber. Your digestive system's regulation and illness prevention depends heavily on fiber. Consuming extra fiber may help you healthily lose weight, reduce your chance of developing diabetes, and boost your good gut flora.

2. Use the Fast Cooking Options

While cooking meat and poultry might take a while, plant-based protein sources can be prepared quickly or even without cooking. You have additional alternatives for preparing fast and wholesome meals now that you can use canned beans, lentils, and fresh fruits and vegetables.

3. Increase nutrient and vitamin intake.

With a plant-based diet, you may add a variety of vitamins without taking additional supplements like pills or drinks. A wide range of vitamins are present in plants such as vegetables, fruits, and other foods. They also provide additional nutrients like fiber and better fats. Additionally, you may get a natural energy boost from the natural sugars in common or exotic fruits without experiencing the negative effects of corn syrup or white sugar.

4. Prevent Illnesses and Conditions

Choosing a plant-based diet may help reduce the risk of contracting certain ailments and diseases, which is another advantage. Studies on people who alter their diets to include other plant-based foods have shown a decreased risk of developing specific malignancies, better cardiovascular responses, lowering blood pressure outcomes, and a decreased risk of weight gain due to diet.

5. Control your Weight

A plant-based diet may assist you in controlling your weight. Your favorite foods may be used to create a broad range of recipes, enabling you to consume whole, nutrient-dense meals that keep you satisfied for longer. Whole foods are more satisfying than many processed alternatives.

1.3   How to change to a diet based on vegetables?

There is a difference between wanting to attempt a plant-based diet and doing it. Many individuals have overwhelming feelings because they are unsure where or how to start. However, adding more vegetables and grains to your diet doesn't have to be difficult. In actuality, switching to a plant-based diet may be simple and delicious.

List every plant you like if you're starting. Produce, seeds, nuts, and grains are a few examples. When making your list, be as thorough as you can. You'll soon realize you own many options for future meal components.

You may have noticed that the best place to shop in the grocery store is the perimeter. Produce, tofu, and yogurt may be found there, but there are also many more excellent choices in the inner aisles. Brown rice, canned lentils, quinoa, frozen fruits, and beans are also available there. Before entering, make a detailed list to ensure you only bring out what you need.

Next, look for online plant-based recipes to learn how to season and taste plants. Tamari and other vegan soy sauces are excellent for dipping, cooking, and marinades. Remember that you may purchase soy sauce that is made legitimately, is vegan-certified, and has no animal components or byproducts. Additionally, it tastes great, so you'll constantly be full.

Keep in mind that starting small is okay. Changes should only be made if they excite you and fit into your lifestyle. When you first start, consider adding an extra serving of plant-based meals to every meal or replacing three or four of your weekly dinners with plant-based alternatives. You'll get there if you explore what helps and the things you like the most.

Chapter 2: The 40-Day Meal Plan

Days	Breakfast	Snack	Lunch	Snack	Dinner
Day 1	Scrambled Avocado and Tofu Sandwich	Cinnamon Oranges	Thai Seitan Vegetable Curry	Spiced Warm Lemon Drink	Black Bean And Bulgur Chili
Day 2	Mixed Berry Bowl	Nori Snack Rolls	Tofu Teriyaki Stir-Fry	Fried Avocados	Green Onion Soup
Day 3	Oatmeal with Figs and Banana	Soothing Tea Drink	Noodles Alfredo with Herby Tofu	Sweet Truffles	Avocado Toast with Chickpeas
Day 4	Chia Strawberry Parfait	Plant-Based Crispy Falafel	Portobello Burger & Veggie Fries	Pleasant Lemonade	Grandma's Creamy Soup
Day 5	Breakfast Potatoes	Banana and Spinach Smoothie	Chickpea, Acorn Squash, and Couscous Soup	Strawberry Blender Pancakes	Garlic Lime Roasted Asparagus
Day 6	Mexican Hot Chocolate	Spinach and Strawberry Salad	Red Kidney Bean Pâté	Caramelize Oven-baked Plantains	Roasted Creamy Beet Soup
Day 7	Nutty Granola alongside Dried Currants	Energizing Detox Ginger Tonic	Bean plus Vegetable Stew	Asparagus and Chickpeas Salad	Teriyaki Eggplant
Day 8	Scrambled Avocado and	Carrot	Piquillo Salsa Verde	Warm Pomegranate	Autumn

	Tofu Sandwich	Fritters	Steak	Punch	Squash Soup
Day 9	Granola	Whole Wheat Chocolate Waffle	Zucchini Meatballs	Orange Parfait	Ribollita or Traditional Tuscan Bean Stew
Day 10	Fruit Salad with Ginger-Lemon Syrup	Rich Truffle Hot Chocolate	Smoked Tempeh & Broccoli Fritters	Mango Smoothie	Green Onion Soup
Day 11	Banana Fluffy Pancakes	Baked Potato	Mexican-Style Chili Soup	Nice Spiced Cherry Cider	Lemon Couscous & Tempeh Kabobs
Day 12	Banana Blueberry Smoothie	Energizing Detox Ginger Tonic	Anasazi Bean Stew	Ultimate Mulled Wine	Thai Seitan Vegetable Curry
Day 13	Fry-bread with Jam and Peanut Butter	Apple Cinnamon Skillet	Chickpeas and Rice	Plant-Based Crispy Falafel	Fresco Sofritas Tacos
Day 14	Cherry Chocolate Smoothie	Pleasant Lemonade	Vegan Chicken & Rice	Whole Wheat Chocolate Waffle	Red Kidney Bean Salad
Day 15	Tasty Oatmeal Muffins	Fruity Smoothie	Roasted Creamy Beet Soup	Cinnamon Oranges	Cheesy Potato Casserole
Day 16	Classic French toast	Balsamic Avocado	Soybean Chinese-	Banana and Spinach	Mushroom Marinated

			Style Salad	Smoothie	Wraps
Day 17	Omelet with Chickpea Flour	Asparagus and Chickpeas Salad	Scalloped Potatoes	Apple Cinnamon Skillet	Noodles Alfredo with Herby Tofu
Day 18	Ciabatta Bread Pudding with Sultanas	Energizing Detox Ginger Tonic	Roasted Cheesy Asparagus	Nice Spiced Cherry Cider	Green Lentil Stew and Collard Greens
Day 19	Nutty Oatmeal Morning Muffins	Banana and Spinach Smoothie	Green Onion and Mushroom Stir-Fry	Plant-Based Crispy Falafel	Chickpea, Acorn Squash, and Couscous Soup
Day 20	Vegan Banh Mi	Fragrant Spiced Coffee	The Tempeh Chili	Whole Wheat Chocolate Waffle	Basic Amaranth Porridge
Day 21	Pepper and Scallion Omelet	Strawberry Blender Pancakes	Spinach Casserole	Carrot Fritters	Creamy Rutabaga Soup
Day 22	White Sandwich Bread	Orange Parfait	Old-Fashioned Vegetable and Lentil Stew	Avocado Toast with Flaxseeds	Lime Pasta
Day 23	Scrambled Avocado and Tofu	Energizing Detox Ginger Tonic	Everyday Savory Grits	Balsamic Avocado	Cannellini Bean Soup and Kale

	Sandwich			
Day 24	A Toast to Remember	Warm Pomegranate Punch	Amaranth Vegetable Soup	Rich Truffle Hot Chocolate	Mushroom Patties with Herbs
Day 25	Banana Fluffy Pancakes	Mango Smoothie	The Tempeh Chili	Spinach and Strawberry Salad	Golden Creamy Veggie Soup
Day 26	Morning Oats with Currants and Walnuts	Carrot Fritters	Stuffed peppers	Fried Avocados	Greek-Style Tomato and Pinto Bean Soup
Day 27	Breakfast Potatoes	Plant-Based Crispy Falafel	Cream of Carrot Soup	Energizing Detox Ginger Tonic	Rye Porridge with Blueberry Topping
Day 28	Tasty Panini	Caramelize Oven-baked Plantains	Coconut Sorghum Porridge	Warm Pomegranate Punch	Portobello Burger & Veggie Fries
Day 29	Mixed Berry Bowl	Asparagus and Chickpeas Salad	Winter Root Vegetable Soup	Strawberry Blender Pancakes	Zucchini Meatballs
Day 30	Classic Applesauce Pancakes and Coconut	Pleasant Lemonade	Chipotle Roasted Chickpeas	Carrot Fritters	Tofu Teriyaki Stir-Fry
Day 31	Classic French toast	Orange Parfait	Smoked Tempeh & Broccoli Fritters	Nori Snack Rolls	Mom's Millet Muffins

Day 32	Mushroom and Onion Tart	Rich Truffle Hot Chocolate	Potato Creamed Soup with Herbs	Banana and Spinach Smoothie	Lime pasta
Day 33	Easy Morning Polenta	Warm Pomegranate Punch	Cornmeal Porridge with Maple Syrup	Asparagus and Chickpeas Salad	Mushroom Tomato Spaghetti Squash
Day 34	Banana-Cinnamon French Toast	Fried Avocados	Potato Soup	Asparagus and Chickpeas Salad	Mushroom Marinated Wraps
Day 35	Pepper and Scallion Omelet	Soothing Tea Drink	Millet Porridge with Sultanas	Whole Wheat Chocolate Waffle	Cream of Carrot Soup
Day 36	Indian Traditional Roti	Baked Potato	Cauliflower Steak Kicking Corn	Sweet Truffles	Spinach Casserole
Day 37	Classic Tofu Scramble	Carrot Fritters	Cucumber and Avocado Soup	Apple Cinnamon Skillet	Eggplant Stacks
Day 38	Chia Chocolate Pudding	Asparagus and Chickpeas Salad	Scalloped Potatoes	Fried Avocados	Quinoa Porridge with Dried Figs
Day 39	Granola	Nori Snack Rolls	Sweet Maize Easy Meal Porridge	Cinnamon Oranges	Vegan Chicken & Rice

Day 40	Easy Morning Polenta	Warm Pomegranate Punch	Amaranth Vegetable Soup	Orange Parfait	Mushroom Tomato Spaghetti Squash

Chapter 3: Breakfast Recipes

Below are the recipes.

1. Scrambled Avocado and Tofu Sandwich

(Preparation Time: 15 minutes | Cooking Time: 10 minutes | Serving 2 | Difficulty: Easy)

Ingredients:

- 5 ounces extra-firm tofu, crumbled and pressed
- 4 slices of rye bread
- ½ avocado, medium-sized peeled, pitted, and sliced
- 1 cucumber, small-sized sliced
- 1 tablespoon olive oil
- ½ teaspoon turmeric powder
- 1 tablespoon spicy mustard
- 1 tomato, medium-sized sliced
- Salt and ground black pepper, for season

Instructions:

1. In a frying pan, heat the olive oil over medium-high heat. Add the tofu when heated and simmer for about 8 minutes, stirring regularly to ensure equal cooking.
2. After adding it, add your turmeric powder and cook for another minute or two.
3. On each slice of bread, spread the hot mustard.
4. Divide your tofu scramble among the two slices of bread, then top with the tomatoes, avocado, and cucumber. Add salt and black pepper to taste.
5. Serve the sandwiches after sealing them with the leftover bread pieces. Enjoy!

Nutritional Info: Calories: 363 kcal, Protein: 13.6g, Carb: 35.4g, Fat: 20.3g.

2. Chia Strawberry Parfait

(Preparation Time: 10 minutes | Cooking Time: 10 minutes | Serving 2 | Difficulty: Easy)

Ingredients:

- 3 tablespoons chia seeds
- 3 tablespoon maple syrup
- 3 ounces strawberry, sliced
- 2 ½ tablespoons coconut, shredded and unsweetened
- 6 ounces almond milk, unsweetened

Additional:

- ½ teaspoon unsweetened vanilla extract

Instructions:

1. Chia and coconut should be blended with maple syrup, milk, and vanilla in a medium bowl. Chia and coconut should also be combined with the other ingredients.

2. After allowing the mixture to sit for 30 minutes, whisk it and chill it for at least three hours or overnight.

3. When ready to serve, spread half of your chia mixture into the bottom of a serving glass, top with an equal layer of three-fourths of the strawberry slices, sprinkle the remaining chia seeds on top, and then serve.

4. Serve immediately.

5. As instructed in recipes, layer parfait in wide-mouth pint jars, seal snugly with lids, and keep the jars in the fridge for up to 7 days. Take a bite of it cold when you're ready.

Nutritional Info: Calories: 220 kcal, Protein: 31g, Carb: 7.1g, Fat: 3.3g.

3. Mixed Berry Bowl

(Preparation Time: 10 minutes | Cooking Time: 10 minutes | Serving 2 | Difficulty: Easy)

Ingredients:

- 2 bananas, small-sized

- 2 tablespoons almond butter

- 2 tablespoons granola

- 1 ½ cups coconut milk

- 1 cup berries, frozen mixed

- 1 tablespoon chia seeds

Instructions:

1. Bananas, almond butter, berries, chia seeds, and coconut milk should all be included.

2. Blend until smooth, consistent, and creamy.

3. Distribute the combined mixture into serving dishes, and then sprinkle granola.

4. Serve right away.

Nutritional Info: Calories: 533 kcal, Protein: 6.9g, Carb: 43.4g, Fat: 42.3g.

4. Mexican Hot Chocolate

(Preparation Time: 5 minutes | Cooking Time: 5 minutes | Serving 2 | Difficulty: Easy)

Ingredients:

- 1 teaspoon ground cinnamon, ground

- ½ teaspoon unsweetened vanilla extract

- 2 tablespoons maple syrup

- 2 tablespoons cocoa powder

- 2 cups unsweetened almond milk

Additional:

- 1/3 teaspoon nutmeg, ground

Instructions:

1. Take a small saucepan, heat it to medium-low, add all the ingredients, and then whisk until everything is well combined.

2. Remove the saucepan after cooking for four to five minutes to ensure it is heated.

3. Divide the remaining ingredients among the mini-meal prep cups, add the lid, and then divide the milk among the Mason jars. For up to 7 days, keep the milk and additional ingredients in the fridge. When you're ready to consume it, make the hot chocolate as directed in the recipe above, and then dispense.

Nutritional Info: Calories: 110 kcal, Protein: 17.4g, Carb: 17.4g, Fat: 3g.

5. Oatmeal with Figs and Banana

(Preparation Time: 5 minutes | Cooking Time: 12 minutes | Serving 2 | Difficulty: Easy)

Ingredients:

- ½ cup rolled oats
- A pinch of nutmeg, grated
- 3 figs, dried chopped
- 1 tablespoon maple syrup
- 1 ½ cups almond milk
- A pinch of sea salt
- 1/3 teaspoon cinnamon
- 2 bananas, sliced and peeled

Instructions:

1. Bring your milk to a rolling boil in a large pot. Oats are added, the pan is covered, and the heat is medium.

2. Add the cinnamon, nutmeg, and salt. Cook for another 12 minutes or so, stirring occasionally.

3. Place the mixture in serving dishes, top with bananas and figs, drizzle each bowl with a little maple syrup, and serve warm. Good appetite!

Nutritional Info: Calories: 404 kcal, Protein: 9g, Carb: 84g, Fat: 5.4g.

6. Breakfast Potatoes

(Preparation Time: 5 minutes | Cooking Time: 8 minutes | Serving 2 | Difficulty: Easy)

Ingredients:

- 1 chopped green onion

- 1 teaspoon oregano, dried

- 8 ounces of potatoes, diced

- 1/3 teaspoon salt

- 1 ½ tablespoon olive oil

Additional:

- ½ teaspoon cumin

- ¼ teaspoon black pepper, ground

Instructions:

1. Once the oil is heated, add the potatoes, stir, and cook for about 2 minutes in a medium skillet over medium heat.

2. Add salt, cumin, oregano, and pepper. Stir to combine. Cook for an additional 3 to 4 minutes or until done.

3. Add some green onions, and then serve.

4. Potatoes should be divided into two meal prep containers and covered when cooled.

5. When ready to eat, warm potatoes in the microwave for 1 to 2 minutes until hot, then serve. Potatoes may be stored in the refrigerator for over five to seven days.

Nutritional Info: Calories: 178 kcal, Protein: 18.7g, Carb: 10g, Fat: 2.2g.

7. Nutty Granola alongside Dried Currants

(Preparation Time: 5 minutes | Cooking Time: 20 minutes | Serving 12 | Difficulty: Moderate)

Ingredients:

- 1/3 cup maple syrup

- ½ teaspoon cardamom, ground

- 1/3 teaspoon Himalayan salt

- ½ cup chopped pecans

- ¼ cup pepitas

- ½ cup coconut oil

- 1 teaspoon vanilla paste

- 1 teaspoon cinnamon, ground

- 4 cups oats, old-fashioned

- ½ cup chopped walnuts

- 1 cup currants, dried

Instructions:

1. Set your oven at 290 degrees Fahrenheit and cover a big baking sheet with parchment paper to get started.

2. Then, completely blend the Himalayan salt, cardamom, vanilla paste, maple syrup, and coconut oil.

3. The nuts, oats, and seeds should be added gradually. Toss to coat evenly.

4. The prepared baking sheet should be covered with the mixture.

5. Cook for approximately 20 minutes in the center of your oven, stirring once halfway through or until golden brown.

6. Before storing, stir your granola and add the dried currants.

7. Use an airtight container for storage.

8. Serve with your preferred plant-based yogurt or milk. Good appetite!

Nutritional Info: Calories: 374 kcal, Protein: 10.5g, Carb: 43.2g, Fat: 19.1g.

8. Fruit Salad with Ginger-Lemon Syrup

(Preparation Time: 10 minutes | Cooking Time: 10 minutes | Serving 4 | Difficulty: Easy)

Ingredients:

- ¼ cup agave syrup
- ½ teaspoon vanilla extract
- 2 cups berries, mixed
- 2 cups apples, diced and cored
- ½ cup lemon juice, fresh
- 1 teaspoon ginger, fresh grated
- 1 sliced banana
- 1 cup seedless grapes

Instructions:

1. Over medium-high heat, bring the agave syrup, lemon juice, and ginger to a boil. When it has somewhat thickened, reduce the heat to medium to low and allow it to simmer for approximately 6 minutes.
2. Add the vanilla essence after turning the heat off. Give it time to cool.
3. Put the fruits inside serving basins in layers. Place the fruit on a serving dish and top with the cooled sauce. Good appetite!

Nutritional Info: Calories: 164 kcal, Protein: 1.4g, Carb: 42g, Fat: 0.5g.

9. Granola

(Preparation Time: 5 minutes | Cooking Time: 8 minutes | Serving 2 | Difficulty: Easy)

Ingredients:

- ½ cup almonds, sliced
- ¼ teaspoon unsweetened vanilla extract
- ½ cup coconut, shredded

- ½ tablespoon coconut sugar

- 2 tablespoons coconut oil

Instructions:

1. Turn on the oven, lower the temperature to 300 degrees F and let it warm.

2. To melt it, coconut oil should be placed in a small bowl and heated in the microwave for at least 30 seconds.

3. Almonds and coconut should be combined in a medium bowl with a sprinkle of oil.

4. Spread the granola mixture evenly over the bottom of a baking sheet, spray it with oil, and bake for 5 to 7 minutes or until the coconut is golden brown.

5. When finished, let the granola cool before serving.

6. Place the granola in an airtight jar and cover using a lid once it has cooled. When you're ready to dine, serve.

Nutritional Info: Calories: 468.5 kcal, Protein: 7g, Carb: 18.7g, Fat: 40.6g.

10. Banana Fluffy Pancakes

(Preparation Time: 15 minutes | Cooking Time: 10 minutes | Serving 4 | Difficulty: Easy)

Ingredients:

- ½ cup oat flour

- ½ cup instant oats

- ¼ teaspoon kosher salt

- ¼ teaspoon cinnamon, ground

- 1 cup banana

- 2 tablespoons flaxseeds, ground

- ½ cup coconut flour

- 1 teaspoon baking powder

- ¼ teaspoon cardamom, ground

- ½ teaspoon coconut extract

- 2 tablespoons coconut oil, available at room temperature

Instructions:

1. To prepare the "flax" egg, combine 2 teaspoons of ground flaxseed and 4 tablespoons of water inside a small mixing bowl. Give it a minimum of 15 minutes to sit.

2. Mix the oats, flour, baking soda, and spices well in a mixing dish. Add the mashed banana and flax egg. Stir everything together well.

3. Warm up ½ tablespoon coconut oil in a frying pan over low heat. Around ¼ cup of your batter should be poured into the frying pan; cook your pancake for three minutes on each side.

4. Continue until the batter is finished. Enjoy when serving with your favorite toppings!

Nutritional Info: Calories: 302 kcal, Protein: 7.1g, Carb: 37.2g, Fat: 15g.

11. Fry-bread with Jam and Peanut Butter

(Preparation Time: 5 minutes | Cooking Time: 18 minutes | Serving 3 | Difficulty: Easy)

Ingredients:

- ½ teaspoon baking powder
- 1 teaspoon coconut sugar
- 3 teaspoon olive oil
- 3 tablespoons raspberry jam
- 1 cup flour, all-purpose
- ½ teaspoon sea salt
- ½ cup warm water
- 3 tablespoons peanut butter

Instructions:

1. Mix the flour, salt, baking powder, and sugar well. Add the water a little at a time once the dough mixes.

2. The dough should be divided into three equal balls. Flatten every ball to form circles.

27

3. Warm 1 teaspoon of olive oil in a frying pan over medium heat. Cook the first loaf of bread until golden brown, approximately 9 minutes. Continue by using the leftover dough and oil.

4. Serve your fry bread with raspberry jam and peanut butter. Enjoy!

Nutritional Info: Calories: 293 kcal, Protein: 5.5g, Carb: 50.3g, Fat: 7.8g.

12. Banana Blueberry Smoothie

(Preparation Time: 5 minutes | Cooking Time: 0 minutes | Serving 2 | Difficulty: Easy)

Ingredients:

- 3 ounces blueberry

- ½ teaspoon unsweetened vanilla extract

- 2 sliced bananas

- 1 teaspoon cinnamon, ground

- 1 cup unsweetened almond milk

Additional:

- ¾ cup of ice cubes

- ½ cup water

Instructions:

1. In a blender or food processor, combine all the ingredients in the specified order and pulse for 1 to 2 minutes or until smooth.

2. The blender should be divided between two glasses before being served.

3. Smoothies should be divided into two jars or bottles, covered with a lid, and kept in the refrigerator for up to three days.

Nutritional Info: Calories: 79 kcal, Protein: 1g, Carb: 18.4g, Fat: 1.6g.

13. Classic French toast

(Preparation Time: 5 minutes | Cooking Time: 15 minutes | Serving 2 | Difficulty: Easy)

Ingredients:

- 1 cup coconut milk

- A pinch of sea salt

- ½ teaspoon cinnamon, ground

- 1 tablespoon agave syrup

- 1 tablespoon flax seeds, ground

- ½ teaspoon vanilla paste

- A pinch of nutmeg, grated

- ¼ teaspoon cloves, ground

- 4 slices of bread

Instructions:

1. Mix the vanilla, flax seeds, salt, coconut milk, nutmeg, cloves, cinnamon, and agave syrup well in a mixing dish.

2. After being dredged in the milk mixture, every bread slice should be well covered on both sides.

3. An electric grill should be gently oiled with nonstick cooking spray and heated to medium heat.

4. On the hot grill, toast each piece of bread for approximately 3 minutes on each side or until golden brown.

5. Good appetite!

Nutritional Info: Calories: 233 kcal, Protein: 8.2g, Carb: 35.5g, Fat: 6.5g.

14. Ciabatta Bread Pudding with Sultanas

(Preparation Time: 10 minutes | Cooking Time: 2 hours | Serving 4 | Difficulty: Hard)

Ingredients:

- ½ cup agave syrup
- ½ teaspoon vanilla essence
- ¼ teaspoon cloves, ground
- ¼ teaspoon Himalayan salt
- ½ cup sultana raisins
- 2 cups coconut milk, unsweetened
- 1 tablespoon coconut oil
- ½ teaspoon cardamom, ground
- ½ teaspoon cinnamon, ground
- ¾ pound stale cubed ciabatta bread

Instructions:

1. Coconut milk, coconut oil, agave syrup, vanilla, crushed cloves, cardamom, Himalayan salt, and cinnamon combine in a mixing bowl.

2. Stir thoroughly after adding the bread squares to the custard mixture. After folding the sultana raisins, let the mixture rest on a counter for approximately an hour.

3. Then, spoon the mixture inside a casserole dish that has been gently greased.

4. Bake for approximately an hour at 350 degrees Fahrenheit in the oven or once the top becomes golden brown.

5. Before slicing and serving, let the bread pudding sit on your wire rack for about 10 minutes. Good appetite!

Nutritional Info: Calories: 379 kcal, Protein: 21g, Carb: 16g, Fat: 25g.

15. Cherry Chocolate Smoothie

(Preparation Time: 5 minutes | Cooking Time: 0 minutes | Serving 2 | Difficulty: Easy)

Ingredients:

- 2 ounces Medjool dates
- 1 cup unsweetened almond milk
- 2 ounces cherries
- 2 tablespoons almond butter
- ½ cup of water

Additional:

- ¾ cup ice cubes

Instructions:

1. In a blender or food processor, combine all the ingredients in the specified order and pulse for 1 to 2 minutes or until smooth.

2. The blender should be divided between two glasses before being served.

3. Smoothies may be divided between two bottles or jars, sealed with a lid, and kept inside the refrigerator for three days.

Nutritional Info: Calories: 210.5 kcal, Protein: 3.7g, Carb: 27.9g, Fat: 9.4g.

16.   Tasty Oatmeal Muffins

(Preparation Time: 10 minutes | Cooking Time: 20 minutes | Serving 12 | Difficulty: Easy)

Ingredients:

- ½ cup of raisins
- 2 cups of rolled oats
- ½ cup of walnuts
- 1 banana
- ¼ cup of maple syrup
- ½ cup of hot water
- ¼ cup flaxseed, ground

- ¼ teaspoon of sea salt

- ¼ teaspoon of baking soda

- 2 tablespoons of cinnamon

Instructions:

1. Water and flaxseed are whisked together, and the mixture is given approximately five minutes to rest.

2. Blend all the ingredients in a food processor, including the flaxseed mixture. 30 seconds of blending should not result in a smooth mixture. You need a semi-coarse batter to make cookies with a rough texture.

3. Place the batter-lined cupcake liners in a muffin tray. You will require cupcake liners since this recipe does not call for oil. At 350 degrees, bake the ingredients for around 20 minutes.

4. Enjoy the freshly baked cookies with a nice milk beverage.

Nutritional Info: Calories: 133 kcal, Protein: 3g, Carb: 27g, Fat: 2g.

17. Vegan Banh Mi

(Preparation Time: 30 minutes | Cooking Time: 30 minutes | Serving 4 | Difficulty: Hard)

Ingredients:

- ¼ cup water

- 2 carrots, chopped into 1/16-inch matchsticks

- 1 thinly sliced white onion

- 12 ounces firm tofu, chopped into sticks

- 1 ½ tablespoons soy sauce

- ¼ cup fresh chopped parsley

- 2 standard French baguettes, chopped into 4 pieces

- 4 lime wedges

- ½ cup rice vinegar

- ¼ cup white sugar

- ½ cup daikon white radish chopped into 1/16 inch matchsticks

- 2 tablespoons olive oil

- ¼ cup vegan mayonnaise

- 2 minced cloves garlic

- Ground black pepper and kosher salt, for taste

- 4 tablespoons cilantro, fresh chopped

Instructions:

1. Rice vinegar, sugar, and water are brought to a boil while stirring for approximately a minute. Give it time to cool.

2. Pour the vinegar mixture on the carrot, onion, and daikon radish when it has cooled, and let the veggies at least 30 minutes to marinate.

3. Warm the olive oil while the veggies marinate inside a frying pan at medium to high heat. When the pan is heated, add all tofu and simmer for 8 minutes, turning regularly to ensure equal cooking.

4. Combine the mayonnaise, garlic, soy sauce, salt, parsley, and freshly ground black pepper in a small bowl.

5. Cut each baguette slice in half lengthwise. Then, roast the baguette halves for approximately 3 minutes under the preheated broiler.

6. Spread the mayonnaise mixture over both halves of the toasted baguette before stuffing the hollow of the bottom half of your bread with fried marinated veggies, tofu sticks, and cilantro leaves to make the banh mi sandwiches.

7. Then, top with some other half of your baguette and squeeze the lime wedges over the contents. Good appetite!

Nutritional Info: Calories: 372 kcal, Protein: 17.6g, Carb: 29.5g, Fat: 21.9g.

18. Omelet with Chickpea Flour

(Preparation Time: 10 minutes | Cooking Time: 20 minutes | Serving 1 | Difficulty: Easy)

Ingredients:

- ¼ teaspoon black pepper

- ½ teaspoon garlic powder

- ¼ teaspoon white pepper

- 3 green onions, finely chopped

- ½ teaspoon onion powder

- 1 cup chickpea flour

- ½ teaspoon baking soda

- 1/3 cup nutritional yeast

- 4 ounces mushrooms, sautéed

Instructions:

1. Combine the nutritional yeast, baking soda, garlic powder, onion powder, black and white pepper, white pepper, and chickpea flour in a small bowl.

2. Make a smooth batter by adding 1 cup of water.

3. Place a frying pan on medium heat, add the batter, and cook it like pancakes.

4. Sprinkle some mushrooms and green onions on the batter. Cook the omelet on both sides equally.

5. Serve your omelet with salsa, tomatoes, spinach, spicy sauce, and both sides.

Nutritional Info: Calories: 150 kcal, Protein: 10.2g, Carb: 24.4g, Fat: 1.9g.

19.   Nutty Oatmeal Morning Muffins

(Preparation Time: 10 minutes | Cooking Time: 20 minutes | Serving 9 | Difficulty: Easy)

Ingredients:

- ½ cup coconut shredded unsweetened

- ¼ teaspoon salt

- ¼ teaspoon coconut extract

- ½ teaspoon cardamom

- 1/3 cup pumpkin, canned

- ¼ cup golden raisins

- 1 ½ cups rolled oats

- ¾ teaspoon baking powder

- ¼ teaspoon vanilla extract

- ¼ teaspoon nutmeg, grated

- ¾ cup coconut milk

- ¼ cup agave syrup

- ¼ cup chopped pecans

Instructions:

1. Start by setting the oven to 360 degrees Fahrenheit. Spray non-stick cooking oil in a muffin pan.

2. Mix all the ingredients well in a bowl beside the pecans and raisins.

3. Scrape all batter into your prepared muffin tray after incorporating the pecans and raisins.

4. The tops of your muffins should be set after 25 minutes of baking.

Nutritional Info: Calories: 192 kcal, Protein: 5.6g, Carb: 30.5g, Fat: 6g.

20. White Sandwich Bread

(Preparation Time: 10 minutes | Cooking Time: 20 minutes | Serving 16 | Difficulty: Moderate)

Ingredients:

- 2 tablespoons active dry yeast

- 2 ½ teaspoons salt

- 1 cup almond milk warm or other non-dairy milk, any as your preference

- 6 cups flour, all-purpose

- 1 cup warm water

- 4 tablespoons oil

- 2 tablespoons raw sugar or 4 tablespoons agave nectar/maple syrup

Instructions:

1. Stir together the yeast, warm water, and sugar in a basin. Place aside for five minutes until a frothy mass of many small bubbles has formed.

2. In a mixing dish, combine the salt and flour. Mix the milk, oil, and yeast mixture into the dough. When the dough is too stiff, add a tablespoon of water at one time and mix thoroughly after each addition. A spoonful at a time, add extra flour while the dough becomes too sticky. The dough should be soft and elastic after 8 minutes of kneading. You may use your hands or the stand mixer's dough hook attachment.

3. Spray a few drops of water on the dough now. Maintain a cloth covering over the bowl. As soon as it doubles in size, let it rest.

4. Place the dough on your countertop after removing it from the bowl.

5. Roll out the dough.

6. Using parchment paper, line a loaf pan. If you'd like, you may also lubricate with olive oil. If you want to bake smaller loaves, as I did, you may use two smaller loaf pans.

7. In the loaf pan, put the dough. Now spritz the dough with extra water. Keeps a cloth covering the loaf pan? Allow the dough to rest until it has doubled in size.

8. For around 40 to 50 minutes, bake at 370° F in a preheated oven until a toothpick inserted in the middle of the bread kneads out clean.

9. Wait until it reaches room temperature.

10. Slice into 16 equal pieces, then use as needed. Store at room temperature in a breadbox.

Nutritional Info: Calories: 209 kcal, Protein: 1g, Carb: 35g, Fat: 4g.

21. Chia and Raspberry Smoothie Bowl

(Preparation Time: 10 minutes | Cooking Time: 10 minutes | Serving 2 | Difficulty: Easy)

Ingredients:

- 2 bananas, small-sized and peeled

- 2 pitted dates

- 1 tablespoon pepitas

- 1 cup coconut milk

- 1 ½ cups raspberries, frozen or fresh

- 1 tablespoon coconut flakes

- 2 tablespoons chia seeds

Instructions:

1. Bananas, dates, raspberries, and coconut milk should all be combined in a food processor or blender.

2. Process until smooth and creamy. Place the smoothie in each of the two bowls.

3. Chia seeds, pepitas, and coconut flakes are sprinkled on each smoothie bowl.

Nutritional Info: Calories: 442 kcal, Protein: 9.6g, Carb: 85g, Fat: 10.9g.

22. A Toast to Remember

(Preparation Time: 10 minutes | Cooking Time: 15 minutes | Serving 4 | Difficulty: Easy)

Ingredients:

- A pinch of sea salt

- ¼ teaspoon of chipotle spice

- 1 teaspoon of garlic powder

- 1 avocado, freshly diced

- 3 tablespoons onion, finely diced

- Fresh cilantro

- 1 tin of black beans

- 2 pieces of toast, whole-wheat

- A pinch of black pepper

- 1 lime, freshly juiced

- ¼ cup of corn

- ½ tomato, freshly diced

Instructions:

1. Combine the salt, beans, pepper, garlic powder, and chipotle spice in a bowl. Add the lime juice and stir.

2. Everything should be boiled until you get a thick, starchy mixture.

3. Combine the corn, avocado, tomato, cilantro, red onion, and lime juice in a bowl. Add some salt and pepper.

4. Spread the avocado mixture first, then the black bean mixture, on the toast.

5. Enjoy a healthy taste of deliciousness!

Nutritional Info: Calories: 290 kcal, Protein: 12g, Carb: 44g, Fat: 9g.

23. Morning Oats with Currants and Walnuts

(Preparation Time: 10 minutes | Cooking Time: 10 minutes | Serving 2 | Difficulty: Easy)

Ingredients:

- 1 ½ cups oat milk

- A pinch of salt

- ¼ teaspoon cardamom

- 4 tablespoons currants, dried

- 1 cup water

- 1 ½ cups rolled oats

- A pinch of nutmeg, grated

- 1 handful of walnuts, roughly chopped

Instructions:

1. Bring the water and milk to a roaring boil in a large pot. Oats are added, the pan is covered, and the heat is medium.

2. Nutmeg, salt, and cardamom should be added. Twelve to thirteen minutes additional of cooking time should be added, periodically stirring.

3. Place the combination into serving dishes and garnish with currants and walnuts.

Nutritional Info: Calories: 442 kcal, Protein: 9.6g, Carb: 85g, Fat: 10.9g.

24. Tasty Panini

(Preparation Time: 5 minutes | Cooking Time: 0 minutes | Serving 1 | Difficulty: Easy)

Ingredients:

- 1 tablespoon cinnamon

- 2 teaspoons cacao powder

- 2 slices of bread, whole-grain

- ¼ cup of hot water

- ¼ cup raisins

- 1 ripe banana

- ¼ cup peanut butter, natural

Instructions:

1. Cinnamon, boiling water, cacao powder, and raisins should all be combined in a bowl.

2. On the toast, apply the peanut butter.

3. Sliced bananas are placed on toast.

4. Spread the raisin mixture over the sandwich after blending it in a blender.

Nutritional Info: Calories: 850 kcal, Protein: 27g, Carb: 112g, Fat: 34g.

25. Classic Applesauce Pancakes and Coconut

(Preparation Time: 10 minutes | Cooking Time: 40 minutes | Serving 8| Difficulty: Moderate)

Ingredients:

- 1 teaspoon baking powder

- ½ teaspoon coconut sugar

- ¼ teaspoon cardamom, ground

- ¾ cup oat milk

- 2 tablespoons coconut oil

- 8 tablespoons pure maple syrup

- 1 ¼ cups flour, whole-wheat

- ¼ teaspoon sea salt

- ¼ teaspoon cloves, ground

- ½ teaspoon cinnamon, ground

- ½ cup unsweetened applesauce

- 8 tablespoons shredded coconut

Instructions:

1. Mix the flour, salt, baking powder, spices, and sugar in a dish. Add the applesauce and milk gradually.

2. A bit of coconut oil is added to a frying pan that is already hot over a fairly high temperature.

3. Pour all batter into your frying pan once it is heated. When bubbles appear, cook for about 3 minutes before flipping it over and cooking for 3 minutes or until the bottom is browned. Repeat with the leftover batter and oil.

4. Serve with maple syrup and coconut flakes.

Nutritional Info: Calories: 208 kcal, Protein: 3.6g, Carb: 33.2g, Fat: 8g.

26. **Mushroom and Onion Tart**

(Preparation Time: 10 minutes | Cooking Time: 55 minutes | Serving 1 | Difficulty: Hard)

Ingredients:

- 1 cup brown rice, short-grain

- ½ teaspoon black pepper, ground

- 1 sweet onion, large

- 1 cup plain milk, non-dairy

- 2 teaspoons soy, low-sodium

- ¼ teaspoon turmeric, ground

- ¼ cup tapioca

- 1 ½ pounds of mushrooms, portabella or button

- 2 ¼ cups water

- 2 teaspoons herbal spice blend

- 7 ounces tofu, extra-firm

- 2 teaspoons onion powder

- 1 teaspoon molasses

- ¼ cup white wine

Instructions:

1. Brown rice should be prepared and put saved for later use.

2. The onions should be thinly sliced and cooked in water until tender. Add the molasses after that and continue to boil for several minutes.

3. The mushrooms are then sautéed in water containing the herbal spice mixture.

4. Add the sherry or white wine after the mushrooms have been cooked and become soft. Everything needs to cook for other more minutes.

5. Blend the milk, arrowroot, tofu, onion powder, and turmeric until smooth.

6. Make a layer of the rice on a pie dish and spread it uniformly to make a crust. Warm rice is preferred over cold rice. With heated rice, the job will be simple. For a uniform crust, you may alternatively use a pastry roller.

7. Press the sides a little bit with your fingertips.

8. Spoon the mushrooms and half of your tofu mixture over the tart dish; with your spoon, level the surface.

9. Onions and the tofu mixture should now be placed on top of the layer. With your spoon, you may once again smooth the surface.

10. Add the black pepper on the top.

11. The pie should be baked at 350°F for around 45 minutes. You may loosely cover it with tin foil toward the end. The crust will stay wet as a result of this.

12. Slice the pie crust when it has had time to cool. There is not possible that you won't like this pie if you appreciate vegetarian cuisine.

Nutritional Info: Calories: 245.3 kcal, Protein: 6.8g, Carb: 18.3g, Fat: 16.4g.

27. Banana-Cinnamon French toast

(Preparation Time: 10 minutes | Cooking Time: 15 minutes | Serving 3 | Difficulty: Easy)

Ingredients:

- ½ cup mashed banana

- ½ teaspoon baking powder

- A pinch of sea salt

- ½ teaspoon allspice, ground

- 6 slices of sourdough bread, day-old

- 2 tablespoons brown sugar

- 1/3 cup coconut milk

- 2 tablespoons chickpea flour

- ½ teaspoon vanilla paste

- 1 tablespoon agave syrup

- A pinch of nutmeg, grated

- 2 sliced bananas

- 1 teaspoon cinnamon, ground

Instructions:

1. Mix the coconut milk, chickpea flour, mashed banana, baking powder, salt, vanilla, allspice, agave syrup, and nutmeg well to create the batter.

2. Each bread slice should be well covered on both sides after being dredged in the batter.

3. An electric grill should be gently oiled with nonstick cooking spray and heated to medium heat.

4. On the hot grill, toast each piece of bread for approximately 3 minutes on each side or until golden brown.

5. Add the cinnamon, brown sugar and bananas as a garnish to the French toast.

Nutritional Info: Calories: 278 kcal, Protein: 6.6g, Carb: 59g, Fat: 2.9g.

28. Indian Traditional Roti

(Preparation Time: 10 minutes | Cooking Time: 25 minutes | Serving 5 | Difficulty: Easy)

Ingredients:

- 1 teaspoon baking powder

- ¾ warm water

- 2 cups bread flour

- ½ teaspoon salt

- 1 cup vegetable oil used in frying

Instructions:

1. Thoroughly combine the salt, baking powder, and flour in a mixing basin.

2. Add the water a little at a time until the dough mix.

3. Five dough balls should be formed; flatten each to form circles.

4. Warm the olive oil over a fairly high heat in a frying pan. The first piece of bread should be fried for approximately ten minutes or once golden brown, flipping it over to ensure equal cooking.

5. With the remaining dough, repeat. Place each roti on a dish covered with paper towels to drain the extra oil.

Nutritional Info: Calories: 413 kcal, Protein: 5.6g, Carb: 38.1g, Fat: 26g.

29. Chia Chocolate Pudding

(Preparation Time: 10 minutes | Chilling Time: overnight | Serving 4 | Difficulty: Easy)

Ingredients:

- 4 tablespoons maple syrup

- A pinch of nutmeg, grated

- ½ teaspoon cinnamon, ground

- 4 tablespoons cocoa powder, unsweetened

- 1 2/3 cups coconut milk

- A pinch of cloves, ground

- ½ cup chia seeds

Instructions:

1. Combine the milk, cocoa powder, spices, and maple syrup until thoroughly combined.

2. Stir one more after adding the chia seeds. Cover the mixture in four jars, and stay in the fridge overnight.

3. Stir using a spoon and serve the next day.

Nutritional Info: Calories: 346 kcal, Protein: 5.5g, Carb: 28.1g, Fat: 26.7g.

30. Easy Morning Polenta

(Preparation Time: 5 minutes | Cooking Time: 20 minutes | Serving 2 | Difficulty: Easy)

Ingredients:

- ½ cup cornmeal

- ¼ teaspoon black pepper, ground for taste

- 2 tablespoons olive oil

- 2 cups vegetable broth

- ½ teaspoon sea salt

- ¼ teaspoon crushed red pepper flakes

Instructions:

1. Bring your vegetable broth to a boil in a medium saucepan over medium-high heat. Add the cornmeal at this point, stirring constantly to avoid lumps.

2. Add red, black, and salt pepper to taste.

3. Lower the temperature to a simmer. Once the mixture has thickened, simmer the mixture for a further 18 minutes while stirring occasionally.

4. Olive oil should now be added to a pot and mixed well.

Nutritional Info: Calories: 306 kcal, Protein: 7.7g, Carb: 32.4g, Fat: 16g.

31. Pepper and Scallion Omelet

(Preparation Time: 10 minutes | Cooking Time: 15 minutes | Serving 2 | Difficulty: Easy)

Ingredients:

- 3 chopped scallions

- 6 tablespoons chickpea flour

- Black pepper and black salt, ground for the season

- 2 tablespoons Italian parsley, freshly chopped

- 2 tablespoons olive oil

- 2 chopped bell peppers

- 10 tablespoons unsweetened rice milk

- 1/3 teaspoon red pepper flakes

Instructions:

1. In a frying pan, heat the olive oil over medium-high heat. When heated, sauté the peppers and scallions for approximately 3 minutes or until they are fragrant and soft.

2. Meanwhile, combine the black pepper, milk, salt, and red pepper flakes with the chickpea flour.

3. The mixture should then be added to your frying pan.

4. For around 4 minutes, cook. When it is ready, flip it over and cook for three to four minutes. Add fresh parsley to the dish.

Nutritional Info: Calories: 269 kcal, Protein: 8.1g, Carb: 22.4g, Fat: 17g.

32. Classic Tofu Scramble

(Preparation Time: 10 minutes | Cooking Time: 15 minutes | Serving 2 | Difficulty: Easy)

Ingredients:

- 6 ounces extra-firm tofu, crumbled and pressed

- Black pepper and sea salt, ground for taste

- ¼ teaspoon cumin powder

- 1 handful of chives, freshly chopped

- 1 tablespoon olive oil

- 1 cup baby spinach

- ½ teaspoon turmeric powder

- ½ teaspoon garlic powder

Instructions:

1. Over medium heat, warm the olive oil inside a frying pan. Add the tofu when heated and simmer for about 8 minutes, stirring regularly to ensure equal cooking.

2. Baby spinach and the aromatics may now be added. Sauté for a further 1 to 2 minutes.

3. Serve heated with fresh chives as a garnish.

Nutritional Info: Calories: 202 kcal, Protein: 14.6g, Carb: 7.5g, Fat: 14.3g.

Chapter 4: Beans and Grains Recipes

Below are the recipes.

1. Black Bean and Bulgur Chili

(Preparation Time: 10 minutes | Cooking Time: 20 minutes | Serving 4 | Difficulty: Easy)

Ingredients:

- 850 grams or 30 ounces of black beans, cooked
- 1 red onion, chopped, peeled
- 1 chipotle pepper inside adobo sauce, diced, deseeded
- 1 teaspoon paprika, smoked
- 1 teaspoon oregano, dried
- 710 ml or 3 cups vegetable broth
- 1 lime, juiced
- 177 grams or ¾ cup bulgur wheat, ground
- 1 red bell pepper, medium diced, cored
- 1 green bell pepper, medium diced, cored
- 1 teaspoon garlic, minced
- 1/8 teaspoon sea salt
- 1 teaspoon cumin, ground
- 1 tablespoon olive oil
- 295 grams or 1 ¼ cups enchilada sauce

For Topping:

- 118 grams or ½ cup cilantro, chopped

Instructions:

1. Once the oil is heated, adds the garlic and onion, season using salt, and sauté for three minutes or until the onion and garlic is tender.

48

2. When the bell peppers are cooked, add them and simmer for another 5 minutes. Then add the rest of the ingredients and toss to combine.

3. The mixture should be heated to a rolling boil before being reduced to a low simmer for ten minutes.

4. After adjusting the seasoning with a taste test, turn off the heat, place a lid on the pot, and allow it to stand for about 10 minutes.

5. Chili should be divided into bowls, and then served with cilantro on top.

Nutritional Info: Calories: 387 kcal, Protein: 6g, Carb: 18.6g, Fat: 6.5g.

2. Red Kidney Bean Pâté

(Preparation Time: 10 minutes | Cooking Time: 10 minutes | Serving 8 | Difficulty: Easy)

Ingredients:

- 1 chopped onion
- 2 minced cloves garlic
- ¼ cup olive oil
- 2 tablespoons parsley, freshly chopped
- Ground black pepper and sea salt, for taste
- 2 tablespoons olive oil
- 1 chopped bell pepper
- 2 cups red kidney beans, drained and boiled
- 1 teaspoon mustard, stone-ground
- 2 tablespoons basil, fresh chopped

Instructions:

1. Olive oil should be heated in a pan over a medium-high flame. Now, sauté the onion, garlic, and pepper for 3 minutes or until barely soft.

2. Blend the remaining ingredients with the sautéed mixture you added to your blender.

3. Blend or mix the ingredients in a food processor until they are smooth and creamy.

Nutritional Info: Calories: 135 kcal, Protein: 1.6g, Carb: 4.4g, Fat: 12.1g.

3. Ribollita or Traditional Tuscan Bean Stew

(Preparation Time: 10 minutes | Cooking Time: 25 minutes | Serving 5 | Difficulty: Easy)

Ingredients:

- 1 leek, medium chopped

- 1 diced zucchini

- 3 garlic cloves, crushed

- Ground black pepper and kosher salt, for taste

- 28-ounce 1 tin tomatoes, crushed

- 15-ounce 2 tins Great Northern beans, drained

- 1 cup crostini

- 3 tablespoons olive oil

- 1 celery with leaves chopped

- 1 sliced Italian pepper

- 2 bay leaves

- 1 teaspoon cayenne pepper

- 2 cups vegetable broth

- 2 cups Lacinato kale, torn into pieces

Instructions:

1. Heat the olive oil in a heavy-bottomed saucepan over medium heat. Once heated, the leek, celery, pepper, and zucchini should be sautéed for around 4 minutes.

2. Sauté the bay leaves and garlic for approximately a minute.

3. Spices, broth, tomatoes, and canned beans should all be added. Allow it to boil for approximately 15 minutes or until well-cooked while stirring periodically.

4. Add the Lacinato kale and cook for 4 more minutes, stirring now and again.

5. Serve with crostini for decoration.

Nutritional Info: Calories: 388 kcal, Protein: 19.5g, Carb: 57.3g, Fat: 10.3g.

4. Red Kidney Bean Salad

(Preparation Time: 20 minutes | Cooking Time: 1 hour | Serving 6 | Difficulty: Moderate)

Ingredients:

- 2 chopped bell peppers
- 3 ounces canned or frozen corn kernels, drained
- 2 cloves garlic, minced
- ½ cup olive oil, extra-virgin
- 2 tablespoons lemon juice, fresh
- 2 tablespoons cilantro, fresh chopped
- 2 tablespoons basil, fresh chopped
- ¾ pound red kidney beans, overnight soaked
- 1 carrot, grated and trimmed
- 3 heaping tablespoons of scallions, chopped
- 1 red chile pepper, sliced
- 2 tablespoons apple cider vinegar
- Ground black pepper and sea salt, for taste
- 2 tablespoons parsley, freshly chopped

Instructions:

1. Bring a new cold water change over your soaked beans to a boil.
2. Boil it for 10 minutes or such. Simmer the food for 50 to 55 minutes or until it is soft.
3. Transfer the beans to a salad dish when they have finished cooling fully.
4. The other ingredients should be added and mixed well.

Nutritional Info: Calories: 443 kcal, Protein: 18.1g, Carb: 52.2g, Fat: 19.2g.

5. Anasazi Bean Stew

(Preparation Time: 10 minutes | Cooking Time: 1 hour | Serving 3 | Difficulty: Easy)

Ingredients:

- 3 cups vegetable broth, roasted

- 1 chopped thyme sprig

- 3 tablespoons olive oil

- 2 celery stalks, chopped

- 2 bell peppers, chopped and seeded

- 2 garlic cloves, minced

- 1 teaspoon cayenne pepper

- 1 cup Anasazi beans, drained and soaked overnight

- 1 bay laurel

- 1 chopped rosemary sprig

- 1 onion, large chopped

- 2 chopped carrots

- 1 green chili pepper, chopped and seeded

- Ground black pepper and sea salt, for taste

- 1 teaspoon paprika

Instructions:

1. Bring all Anasazi beans and stock to a boil in a saucepan. After boiling, lower the temperature to a simmer. Once the herbs have been added, simmer the mixture for around 50 minutes or until soft.

2. Meanwhile, Olive oil is heated over medium-high heat in a heavy-bottomed saucepan. Now, cook the peppers, onion, carrots, and celery for approximately 4 minutes or until soft.

3. Add the garlic and cook for an additional 30 seconds or until fragrant.

4. Cooked beans should be added to the sautéed mixture. Add paprika, cayenne, black pepper,

and salt to taste.

5. For another 10 minutes, simmer, stirring occasionally, or once everything is well cooked.

Nutritional Info: Calories: 444 kcal, Protein: 20.2g, Carb: 58.2g, Fat: 15.8g.

6. Soybean Chinese-Style Salad

(Preparation Time: 10 minutes | Cooking Time: 10 minutes | Serving 4 | Difficulty: Easy)

Ingredients:

- 1 cup arugula
- 1 cup green cabbage, shredded
- ½ teaspoon garlic, minced
- ½ teaspoon deli mustard
- 1 tablespoon rice vinegar
- 2 tablespoons tahini
- 15-ounce 1 tin soybeans, drained
- 1 cup baby spinach
- 1 onion, thinly sliced
- 1 teaspoon ginger, minced
- 2 tablespoons soy sauce
- 1 tablespoon lime juice
- 1 teaspoon agave syrup

Instructions:

1. Mix the soybeans, spinach, arugula, onion, and cabbage in a salad bowl.
2. Whisk the remaining dressing ingredients in a small mixing bowl.
3. Dress your salad, and then serve right away.

Nutritional Info: Calories: 265 kcal, Protein: 18g, Carb: 21g, Fat: 13.7g.

7. Basic Amaranth Porridge

(Preparation Time: 5 minutes | Cooking Time: 30 minutes | Serving 4 | Difficulty: Easy)

Ingredients:

- 1 cup amaranth
- 4 tablespoons agave syrup
- A pinch of nutmeg, grated
- 3 cups water
- ½ cup coconut milk
- A pinch of kosher salt

Instructions:

1. Amaranth is added, and the water is brought to a boil at medium to high heat before being reduced to a simmer.
2. Stir occasionally to keep the amaranth from adhering to the pan's bottom while it cooks for approximately 30 minutes.
3. Add the other ingredients and simmer for 1 to 2 minutes or until well heated.

Nutritional Info: Calories: 261 kcal, Protein: 7.3g, Carb: 49g, Fat: 4.4g.

8. Quinoa Porridge with Dried Figs

(Preparation Time: 10 minutes | Cooking Time: 15 minutes | Serving 3 | Difficulty: Easy)

Ingredients:

- 2 cups almond milk
- A pinch of salt
- ½ teaspoon cinnamon, ground
- ½ cup figs, dried chopped
- 1 cup white quinoa, rinsed
- 4 tablespoons brown sugar
- ¼ teaspoon nutmeg, grated
- ½ teaspoon vanilla extract

Instructions:

1. Combine the quinoa, sugar, almond milk, salt, ground nutmeg, vanilla essence, and ground cinnamon in a saucepan.

2. Over medium-high heat, bring the mixture to a boil. After approximately 20 minutes, reduce the heat to boil and fluff with a fork.

3. Distribute into three serving dishes, and then top with dried figs.

Nutritional Info: Calories: 414 kcal, Protein: 13.8g, Carb: 71.2g, Fat: 9g.

9. Millet Porridge with Sultanas

(Preparation Time: 5 minutes | Cooking Time: 20 minutes | Serving 3 | Difficulty: Easy)

Ingredients:

- 1 cup coconut milk

- ¼ teaspoon nutmeg, grated

- 1 teaspoon vanilla paste

- 2 tablespoons agave syrup

- 1 cup water

- 1 cup millet, rinsed

- ¼ teaspoon cinnamon, ground

- ¼ teaspoon kosher salt

- 4 tablespoons sultana raisins

Instructions:

1. Combine the salt, water, millet, milk, nutmeg, vanilla, and cinnamon in a saucepan. Bring to a boil.

2. After approximately 20 minutes, reduce the heat to a simmer, stir the millet using a fork, and then pour it into individual bowls.

3. Serve with sultanas and agave syrup.

Nutritional Info: Calories: 353 kcal, Protein: 9.8g, Carb: 65.2g, Fat: 5.5g.

10.   Everyday Savory Grits

(Preparation Time: 5 minutes | Cooking Time: 35 minutes | Serving 4 | Difficulty: Easy)

Ingredients:

- 1 sweet onion, chopped

- 4 cups water

- Cayenne pepper and sea salt, for taste

- 2 tablespoons vegan butter

- 1 teaspoon garlic, minced

- 1 cup stone-ground grit

Instructions:

1. Melt the vegan butter in a skillet over medium-high heat. When heated, sauté the onion for three minutes or until soft.

2. Add the garlic, cook for 30 seconds or until fragrant, then set aside.

3. Over a fairly high heat, bring your water to a rolling boil. Add the salt, grits, and pepper, and stir. Simmer the food for approximately 30 minutes, cover it, and let it cook until well heated through.

4. Add the sautéed mixture, and then reheat the dish.

Nutritional Info: Calories: 238 kcal, Protein: 3.7g, Carb: 38.7g, Fat: 6.5g.

11.   Rye Porridge with Blueberry Topping

(Preparation Time: 5 minutes | Cooking Time: 10 minutes | Serving 3 | Difficulty: Easy)

Ingredients:

- 1 cup water

- 1 cup blueberries, fresh

- 6 pitted dates

- 1 cup rye flakes

- 1 cup coconut milk

- 1 tablespoon coconut oil

Instructions:

1. Combine the rye flakes, water, and coconut milk in a large pot. Heat to a boil at medium to high. Simmer the heat for five to six minutes, and then remove from the heat.

2. Puree the dates, coconut oil, and blueberries in a food processor or blender.

3. Pour into three dishes and top with blueberry garnish.

Nutritional Info: Calories: 359 kcal, Protein: 12.1g, Carb: 56.1g, Fat: 11g.

12. Coconut Sorghum Porridge

(Preparation Time: 5 minutes | Cooking Time: 15 minutes | Serving 2 | Difficulty: Easy)

Ingredients:

- 1 cup water
- ¼ teaspoon nutmeg, grated
- ½ teaspoon cinnamon, ground
- 2 tablespoons agave syrup
- ½ cup sorghum
- ½ cup coconut milk
- ¼ teaspoon cloves, ground
- Kosher salt, for taste
- 2 tablespoons coconut flakes

Instructions:

1. Combine the sorghum, milk, cinnamon, nutmeg, cloves, and kosher salt in a saucepan. Simmer, stirring occasionally, for approximately 15 minutes.

2. Pour the porridge into bowls for serving. Add coconut flakes and agave syrup as a garnish.

Nutritional Info: Calories: 289 kcal, Protein: 7.3g, Carb: 57.8g, Fat: 5.1g.

13. Sweet Maize Easy Meal Porridge

(Preparation Time: 10 minutes | Cooking Time: 15 minutes | Serving 2 | Difficulty: Easy)

Ingredients:

- ½ cup maize meal
- ¼ teaspoon salt
- 2 tablespoons almond butter
- 2 cups water
- ¼ teaspoon allspice, ground
- 2 tablespoons brown sugar

Instructions:

1. Bring your water to a boil in a saucepan, add the maize meal gradually, and reduce the heat to a simmer.
2. Salt and crushed allspice are added. Wait 10 minutes before serving.
3. Gently mix in the almond butter and brown sugar after adding them.

Nutritional Info: Calories: 278 kcal, Protein: 3g, Carb: 37.2g, Fat: 12.7g.

14. Mom's Millet Muffins

(Preparation Time: 10 minutes | Cooking Time: 20 minutes | Serving 8 | Difficulty: Moderate)

Ingredients:

- ½ cup millet
- ½ teaspoon salt
- ½ cup melted coconut oil
- ½ teaspoon cinnamon, ground
- A pinch of nutmeg, grated
- 2 cup flour, whole-wheat
- 2 teaspoons baking powder
- 1 cup coconut milk

- ½ cup agave nectar

- ¼ teaspoon cloves, ground

- ½ cup apricots, dried chopped

Instructions:

1. Start by setting the oven to 400 degrees Fahrenheit. Use nonstick oil to sparingly coat a muffin pan.

2. Combine all dry ingredients in a bowl. Prepare the wet ingredients in a separate bowl. Do not over mix your batter; stir the milk mixture into your flour mixture until it is uniformly moistened.

3. Scrape all batter into your prepared muffin cups before incorporating the apricots.

4. A tester placed in the middle of a muffin should come out dry and clean after approximately 15 minutes of baking it in the oven.

5. Before removing it from the mold and serving, let it sit for 10 minutes on the wire rack.

6. Enjoy!

Nutritional Info: Calories: 367 kcal, Protein: 6.5g, Carb: 53.7g, Fat: 15.9g.

15. Cornmeal Porridge with Maple Syrup

(Preparation Time: 10 minutes | Cooking Time: 20 minutes | Serving 4 | Difficulty: Easy)

Ingredients:

- 2 cups almond milk

- 1 vanilla bean

- ½ cup maple syrup

- 2 cups water

- 1 cinnamon stick

- 1 cup yellow cornmeal

Instructions:

1. Bring the almond milk and water to a boil in a small saucepan. Include the vanilla bean and cinnamon stick.

2. Stirring constantly, gradually add the cornmeal; reduce the heat to boil. Simmer it for around 15 minutes.

3. Pour the maple syrup into the heated porridge before serving.

Nutritional Info: Calories: 328 kcal, Protein: 6.6g, Carb: 63.4g, Fat: 4.8g.

Chapter 5: Main Meals

Below are the recipes.

1. Tofu Teriyaki Stir-Fry

(Preparation Time: 10 minutes | Cooking Time: 20 minutes | Serving 4 | Difficulty: Hard)

Ingredients:

For the Sauce:

- 1 ½ tablespoons rice vinegar
- 2 teaspoons cornstarch
- 3 tablespoons soy sauce
- 118 ml or ½ cup water
- 2 tablespoons garlic, minced
- ½ tablespoon ginger, grated
- 59 grams or ¼ cup of coconut sugar
- 1 tablespoon sesame oil

For the Tofu:

- 2 cups asparagus
- 2 teaspoons red chili sauce
- 3 teaspoons olive oil
- 2 tablespoons green onions, chopped
- 397 grams of tofu, pressed and firm
- 1 tablespoon soy sauce

For Serving:

- 946 grams or 4 cups quinoa, cooked

Instructions:

1. Tofu should be prepared by being patted dry and sliced into 1-inch pieces.

2. Tofu cubes should be added in a single layer to a medium frying pan and heated over medium-high heat with 1 teaspoon of oil. The tofu should be cooked for 3 to 4 minutes or until golden brown.

3. Repeat using the leftover tofu cubes after adding 1 teaspoon of oil to the pan and placing the pieces in a big bowl.

4. Meanwhile, make the sauce by combining all ingredients in a small bowl, whisking until smooth, and setting it away until needed.

5. After cooking the tofu, spray the sauces and stir it to coat. Set it aside until use.

6. After thoroughly cleaning the frying pan, reheat it over medium-high heat. Add the remaining oil; when it is hot, add the green onions and asparagus. Cook for 3 minutes or until the asparagus is tender-crisp.

7. Replacing the tofu pieces in the pan, adding the prepared sauce and adjusting the heat to medium, tossing to combine all the ingredients, and cooking for 3 to 5 minutes, or until the sauce thickens.

8. Once the sauce is prepared, taste it to check the flavor before turning off the heat.

9. Serve the quinoa that has been cooked by dividing it among plates, adding the tofu and veggies last.

Nutritional Info: Calories: 411 kcal, Protein: 12g, Carb: 8g, Fat: 11g.

2. Avocado Toast with Chickpeas

(Preparation Time: 5 minutes | Cooking Time: 5 minutes | Serving 2 | Difficulty: Easy)

Ingredients:

- 4 tablespoons tinned chickpeas, liquid reserved
- 1 teaspoon apple cider vinegar
- ½ of avocado, pitted, peeled
- 1 tablespoon lime juice
- 2 slices of toasted bread

Additional:

- ¼ teaspoon salt

- 1 teaspoon olive oil

- ¼ teaspoon paprika

Instructions:

1. A medium skillet pan should be used for this. Heat the oil over medium heat, add chickpeas, and cook for about 2 minutes.

2. Chickpeas should be coated with 1/8 teaspoon each of paprika and salt before the pan is taken off the heat.

3. Use a fork to mash the avocado in a bowl. Add the vinegar and lime juice, and whisk to combine.

4. Bread pieces should be spread with mashed avocado, followed by chickpeas, and then served.

Nutritional Info: Calories: 235 kcal, Protein: 5.8g, Carb: 31.4g, Fat: 9.3g.

3. Portobello Burger & Veggie Fries

(Preparation Time: 45 minutes | Cooking Time: 30 minutes | Serving 4 | Difficulty: Moderate)

Ingredients:

For veggie fries:

- 2 sweet potatoes, julienned and peeled

- 2 tsp olive oil

- Black pepper and salt to taste

- 3 carrots, julienned and peeled

- 1 rutabaga, julienned and peeled

- ¼ tsp paprika

For Portobello burgers:

- ½ tsp salt

- 4 buns, whole-wheat

- ½ cup roasted red peppers, sliced

- 2 tomatoes, medium chopped

- ¼ cup feta cheese, crumbled (optional)

- 2 cups baby salad greens

- 1 minced clove garlic

- 2 tbsp. olive oil

- 4 Portobello mushroom caps

- 2 tbsp. Kalamata olives, pitted and chopped

- ½ tsp oregano, dried

- 1 tbsp. red wine vinegar

- ½ cup hummus to serve

Instructions:

1. Preheat the oven to 400 degrees for the vegetable fries.

2. Combine the rutabaga, sweet potatoes, and carrots on a baking sheet. Season with salt, pepper, paprika, and olive oil. Rub the spice well onto the veggies using your hands. Bake inside the oven for 20 minutes, stirring halfway through, or until the veggies soften.

3. Transfer to a platter when done and serve from there.

4. Referring to the Portobello burgers:

5. A grill pan should be heated to medium heat while the vegetables roast.

6. Salt and garlic should be crushed in a bowl using a spoon. Add 1 tablespoon of olive oil and stir.

7. The garlic mixture should be brushed on both sides of the mushrooms before grilling them for 8 minutes. Transfer to a plate, then reserve.

8. For two minutes, crisp up the buns inside the pan. Discard on a platter.

9. The other ingredients—all save the hummus—should be combined in a dish and distributed among the bun's bottom halves.

10. The burger should be topped with hummus, covered with the tops of the buns, and served with vegetable fries.

Nutritional Info: Calories: 667 kcal, Protein: 13g, Carb: 87g, Fat: 32g.

4. Teriyaki Eggplant

(Preparation Time: 5 minutes | Cooking Time: 15 minutes | Serving 2 | Difficulty: Easy)

Ingredients:

- 1 chopped green onion
- ½ teaspoon garlic, minced
- ½ pound eggplant
- ½ teaspoon ginger, grated
- 1/3 cup soy sauce
- ½ tablespoon apple cider vinegar
- 1 tablespoon coconut sugar
- 1 tablespoon olive oil

Instructions:

1. To make teriyaki sauce, combine ginger, soy sauce, garlic, sugar, and vinegar, in a medium bowl. Whisk the mixture until the sugar is fully dissolved.

2. Cubed eggplant should be added to the teriyaki sauce, mixed thoroughly, and let sit for 10 minutes.

3. When cooking, set a grill pan over medium-high heat, coat it with oil, and add the marinated eggplant once it's hot.

4. Cook the meat for about 3 to 4 minutes on each side, until it is well browned and starting to sear, regularly dripping the extra marinade over the meat as it cooks, then move it to a platter.

5. After serving, top the eggplant with green onion.

Nutritional Info: Calories: 132 kcal, Protein: 4g, Carb: 13.2g, Fat: 7g.

5. Cauliflower Steak Kicking Corn

(Preparation Time: 30 minutes | Cooking Time: 60 minutes | Serving 6 | Difficulty: Easy)

Ingredients:

- 4 scallions, chopped
- ¼ cup vegetable oil
- 2 big cauliflower heads
- 2 teaspoons capers, drained
- 1 red chili, minced
- 2 ears of corn, shucked
- Pepper and salt to taste

Instructions:

1. The oven temperature is set at 375 degrees.
2. 4 cups of water should be brought to a boil using the highest heat setting.
3. Cook the corn in the saucepan for three minutes or until soft.
4. Cut the kernels off the cob after draining and letting the corn cool.
5. In a skillet, heat 2 tablespoons of vegetable oil.
6. Cook the oil and chili pepper together for about 30 seconds.
7. The scallions should then be added and cooked with the chile pepper until tender.
8. Combine the corn and capers in the pan, and simmer for a minute to melt the flavors. Then turn off the heat.
9. In a pan, heat 1 tablespoon of vegetable oil. Once the pan is hot, start adding two to three cauliflower steaks at a time. Add salt to taste, and then sauté for 3 minutes over medium heat or until faintly browned.
10. Repeat step 5 using the leftover cauliflower when it has finished cooking.
11. Put the corn mixture between the cauliflower florets by pressing it in place.
12. For 25 minutes, bake.

13. Enjoy warm servings!

Nutritional Info: Calories: 153 kcal, Protein: 4g, Carb: 15g, Fat: 10g.

6. Mushroom Tomato Spaghetti Squash

(Preparation Time: 30 minutes | Cooking Time: 10 minutes | Serving 4 | Difficulty: Moderate)

Ingredients:

- 2 cups of tomatoes, diced

- 8 ounces of mushrooms, sliced

- ¼ cup of pine nuts, toasted

- 3 tablespoons of olive oil

- 1 pinch of red pepper flakes, if required

- 6 cups or 2 spaghetti squash, cooked

- 4 cloves of garlic, minced

- 1/3 cup of onions or shallots, chopped

- A small handful of basil cut chiffonade, fresh

- Black pepper and kosher salt to taste

- Parmesan cheese (optional)

Instructions:

1. Prepare your spaghetti squash. Remove the seeds and stringy bits when it is cold enough to handle, then slice it in half and serve with two forks. Set aside your squash.

2. In a big sauté pan, heat oil over medium heat. Add the onions and mushrooms and stir continuously for 3–4 minutes. Add the glitter and whisk for one to two minutes or until fragrant. Don't allow gyro to brew.

3. Then, add the tomatoes and keep stirring.

4. Add cooked "spaghetti squash" and stir until the squash is hot and the vegetables are just distributed.

5. Toss with fresh basil and toasted pine nuts. Then season to taste with pepper, kosher salt,

and, if you'd like, a pinch of red pepper flakes.

Nutritional Info: Calories: 379 kcal, Protein: 21g, Carb: 16g, Fat: 25g.

7. Thai Seitan Vegetable Curry

(Preparation Time: 20 minutes | Cooking Time: 15 minutes | Serving 4 | Difficulty: Easy)

Ingredients:

- 4 cups Seitan, diced

- ½ cup onions, diced

- 2 tbsp Thai red curry paste

- 1 cup coconut milk, unsweetened

- 2 cups spinach

- 1 tbsp vegetable oil

- 1 cup mixed bell peppers, sliced

- 1 small head of broccoli, cut into florets

- 1 tsp garlic puree

- 2 tbsp vegetable broth

- Black pepper and salt to taste

Instructions:

1. Seitan should be fried in vegetable oil inside a big pan over medium heat until it becomes a mild shade of dark brown. Add the bell peppers, onions, and broccoli, and simmer for 4 minutes or until tender.

2. Combine the coconut milk 1 tablespoon and the curry paste.

3. Stir in the leftover vegetable broth and coconut milk after cooking for 1 minute. Cook for ten minutes.

4. Season the curry with black pepper and salt, then stir in the spinach to wilt it.

5. With steaming white or brown rice, serve the curry.

Nutritional Info: Calories: 379 kcal, Protein: 21g, Carb: 16g, Fat: 25g.

8. Chipotle Roasted Chickpeas

(Preparation Time: 5 minutes | Cooking Time: 8 minutes | Serving 2 | Difficulty: Easy)

Ingredients:

- ½ of chipotle chili, minced
- 1 teaspoon adobo sauce
- ¼ teaspoon salt
- 1/3 teaspoon cumin powder
- 8 ounces tinned chickpeas, liquid preserved
- 1 tablespoon olive oil
- 1/3 teaspoon red chili powder
- 1/8 teaspoon black pepper, ground

Instructions:

1. Turn on the oven, lower the temperature to 425 degrees F and let it warm.
2. Put all your ingredients in a medium bowl as you wait, except for the chickpeas.
3. Add the chickpeas, mix well, and then distribute them equally on a baking sheet lined with parchment paper.
4. After roasting the chickpeas for about 8 minutes, stirring them halfway through, let them cool, and then serve.

Nutritional Info: Calories: 222 kcal, Protein: 7.2g, Carb: 26.6g, Fat: 9.6g.

9. Garlic Lime Roasted Asparagus

(Preparation Time: 5 minutes | Cooking Time: 10 minutes | Serving 2 | Difficulty: Easy)

Ingredients:

- ½ teaspoon garlic, minced
- 1 tablespoon olive oil
- 8 ounces asparagus
- ¼ of lime, sliced, zested

- 2 tablespoons parmesan cheese, grated

Additional:

- ¼ teaspoon black pepper, ground

- ¼ teaspoon onion powder

- 1/3 teaspoon salt

- 1/8 teaspoon thyme, dried

Instructions:

1. Turn on the oven, then lower the temperature to 425 degrees F and warm it.

2. Spread equally on a medium baking sheet lined with parchment paper.

3. Add 1/2 tbsp oil to the asparagus, then lime zest, black pepper, salt, onion powder, and thyme.

4. Lime slices should be placed on top of the asparagus before baking for 5 minutes with a midway toss.

5. Then spray the remaining oil and garlic mixture over the asparagus, toss to combine, and bake for 2 minutes.

6. When finished, top the asparagus with cheese before serving.

Nutritional Info: Calories: 115 kcal, Protein: 3.3g, Carb: 5.3g, Fat: 8.5g.

10. Piquillo Salsa Verde Steak

(Preparation Time: 30 minutes | Cooking Time: 25 minutes | Serving 8 | Difficulty: Moderate)

Ingredients:

- 18 oz. firm tofu drained

- Pinch of cayenne

- 1 ½ tbsp. sherry vinegar

- 8 piquillo peppers out of a jar, cut into ½ inch strips and drained

- 3 tbsp. capers, chopped and drained

- 4 ½ inch thick slices of ciabatta

- 5 tbsp. olive oil, extra virgin

- ½ teaspoon cumin, ground

- 1 diced shallot

- 3 tbsp. Parsley, finely chopped

Instructions:

1. Slice the tofu into eight rectangles after placing it on a dish to drain any extra moisture.

2. Use the grill pan instead of prepping your grill. Preheat the grill pan if using one.

3. To prepare our salsa verde, combine 3 tablespoons of extra virgin olive oil, cumin, cayenne, vinegar, parsley, shallot, piquillo peppers, and capers in a medium bowl. Use salt and pepper to taste to season.

4. The tofu slices should be dried using a paper towel.

5. Each side should be gently seasoned with salt & pepper and olive oil.

6. Place your bread on the grill and cook it over medium-high heat for approximately 2 minutes.

7. Now, grill your tofu for approximately 3 minutes on each side or until it is well heated.

8. On the platter, arrange the tofu on top of your toasty bread.

9. Serve the tofu with a little spoonful of the salsa verde.

Nutritional Info: Calories: 427 kcal, Protein: 14.2g, Carb: 67.5g, Fat: 14.6 g.

11. Smoked Tempeh & Broccoli Fritters

(Preparation Time: 25 minutes | Cooking Time: 20 minutes | Serving 4 | Difficulty: Easy)

Ingredients:

For flax egg:

- 12 tbsp water

- 4 tbsp flax seed powder

For broccoli fritters:

- 8 oz. tofu cheese

- ½ tsp onion powder

- ¼ tsp black pepper, freshly ground

- 2 cups of rice broccoli

- 3 tbsp plain flour

- 1 tsp salt

- 4¼ oz. vegan butter

For grilled tempeh:

- 1 tbsp soy sauce

- 1 tbsp ginger, grated

- 10 oz. tempeh slices

- 3 tbsp olive oil

- 3 tbsp lime juice, fresh

- Cayenne pepper and salt to taste

For serving:

- 1 cup vegan mayonnaise

- ½ cup salad greens, mixed

- ½ juiced lemon

Instructions:

1. To prepare the smoked tempeh, combine the flax seed powder with the water in a dish and let it sit for five minutes.

2. Olive oil, lime juice, soy sauce, grated ginger, cayenne pepper, and salt should all be combined in a separate bowl. Slices of tempeh are brushed with the mixture.

3. The tempeh should be grilled for 8 minutes on each side until thoroughly smoked and golden brown. Transfer to a platter and keep heated until ready to serve.

4. Combine the broccoli rice, flour, tofu cheese, onion, black pepper, and salt in a medium bowl. The flax egg should be well incorporated before the mixture is used to make 1-inch-

thick patties.

5. Fry the patties until golden brown on each side, about 8 minutes, in a medium pan with the vegan butter melted over medium heat. Take out the fritters and place them on a platter for later.

6. Combine the vegan mayonnaise and lemon juice in a small bowl.

7. Place the salad leaves on serving plates, top with the broccoli fritters and smoked tempeh, then top with the vegan mayonnaise.

Nutritional Info: Calories: 278 kcal, Protein: 18g, Carb: 39.6g, Fat: 7g.

12. Vegan Chicken & Rice

(Preparation Time: 15 minutes | Cooking Time: 3 hours 30 minutes | Serving 8 | Difficulty: Moderate)

Ingredients:

- Pepper and salt to taste

- 2 teaspoons cumin, ground

- 30 oz. black beans

- Pinch cayenne pepper

- ¾ cup radish, sliced thinly

- 8 Tofu thighs

- ½ teaspoon coriander, ground

- 17 oz. brown rice, cooked

- 1 tablespoon olive oil

- 2 cups pico de gallo

- 2 sliced avocados

Instructions:

1. Add salt, coriander, pepper, and cumin to the tofu to season it.

2. Place into a crock pot.

3. Flow the stock in.

4. Cook for three and a half hours on low.

5. A chopping board should contain the tofu.

6. Chicken should be shredded.

7. Pour the cooking liquid over the shredded tofu.

8. With the tofu and the other ingredients on top, serve your rice in bowls.

Nutritional Info: Calories: 470 kcal, Protein: 40g, Carb: 40g, Fat: 17g.

13. Lemon Couscous & Tempeh Kabobs

(Preparation Time: 2 hours 15 minutes | Cooking Time: 2 hours | Serving 4 | Difficulty: Hard)

Ingredients:

For tempeh kabobs:

- 10 oz. tempeh, 1-inch chunks cut

- 1 small yellow squash, 1-inch chunks cut

- 2 tbsp. olive oil

- 8 soaked wooden skewers

- 1 ½ cups of water

- 1 red onion, 1-inch chunks cut

- 1 small green squash, 1-inch chunks cut

- 1 cup barbecue sauce, sugar-free

For lemon couscous:

- 2 cups of water

- ¼ cup parsley, chopped

- ¼ cup cilantro, chopped

- 1 medium avocado, sliced, pitted and peeled

- 1 ½ cups couscous, whole wheat

- Salt to taste

- ¼ mint leaves, chopped

- 1 lemon, juiced

Instructions:

1. Water should be brought to a boil in a medium saucepan over medium heat for the tempeh kabobs.

2. After boiling it, remove it from the heat and add the tempeh. To get the bitterness out of the tempeh, cover it with the lid and steam it for 5 minutes. After, drain the tempeh.

3. After that, add the tempeh and thoroughly coat it with the barbecue sauce in a medium bowl. Put plastic wrap over the bowl and marinate for two hours.

4. Set a grill to 350 degrees after two hours.

5. Until all ingredients are used, alternately thread single pieces of the tempeh, yellow squash, onion, and green squash onto the skewers.

6. Place the skewers on the grill grates, drizzle with some barbecue sauce, and lightly oil the grates with olive oil. Turn the kabobs over after 3 minutes on every side and brush with more barbecue sauce.

7. To serve, transfer to a plate.

8. For the lemon couscous, combine the water, couscous, and salt in a medium dish and steam for 3–4 minutes in the microwave while the kabobs cook. After the bowl has somewhat cooled, remove it from the microwave.

9. Add the lemon juice, cilantro, mint, and parsley.

10. Serve the couscous with the tempeh kabobs and garnish with the avocado slices.

Nutritional Info: Calories: 820 kcal, Protein: 27g, Carb: 110g, Fat: 35g.

14.   Fresco Sofritas Tacos

(Preparation Time: 30 minutes | Cooking Time: 30 minutes | Serving 5 | Difficulty: Moderate)

Ingredients:

- Poblano peppers 2

- ½ cup of onion, diced

- 1 tbsp of oregano leaves, fresh chopped

- ¼ tsp kosher salt

- 1 cup of black beans, reduced sodium rinsed

- 1 tablespoon of cilantro, fresh

- ½ tsp of cumin

- 1 chipotle pepper inside adobo sauce

- 15 3 per serving small corn tortillas, street taco sized

- 12 ounces organic tofu, extra firm

- 1 tablespoon of red wine vinegar

- 1 garlic clove

- 2 tomatoes, chopped

- 4 tsps. of olive oil, extra virgin divided

- 5 single packets guacamole or substitute avocado

- 1 14 ½ ounces of tin tomatoes, drained and diced

- 5 lime wedges

Instructions:

1. Tofu should be laid out with paper towels and placed under a pot or book for approximately 20 minutes to release moisture.

2. Roast the poblano peppers on the grill, turning them often to get the skin all blistered and black. It may also be carried out using a flashlight. Once finished, transfer them to a large zip-top bag, seal it, and let them steam. When the skin and eyes are cold enough to handle,

remove them. Put one pepper in the food processor. Crush the second pepper and set it aside.

3. Add 1 teaspoon of olive oil to the diced, dried tomatoes and spread them on a baking sheet. Roast for approximately 30 minutes, or until just charred, on a grill set to indirect fire or in an oven set to 400°F. Go to the food processor.

4. To the food processor, add cumin, roasted tomatoes, one of the poblano peppers, garlic, oregano, salt, chipotle pepper, red wine vinegar, and one teaspoon of olive oil, up till smooth process.

5. Heat the last 2 tablespoons of olive oil in a large nonstick pan over high heat. Add the tofu, and cook, turning often and breaking into small pieces with a spatula, until well browned.

6. Add the black beans, chipotle-poblano-tomato sauce, and the reserved diced poblano pepper to the brewed tofu. To five containers, portion out. Add fresh cilantro and tomato on top. Serve corn tortillas with guava and a squeeze of lime.

Nutritional Info: Calories: 320 kcal, Protein: 16g, Carb: 36g, Fat: 14g.

15. Roasted Cheesy Asparagus

(Preparation Time: 5 minutes | Cooking Time: 10 minutes | Serving 2 | Difficulty: Easy)

Ingredients:

- 1 1/3 tablespoon yeast

- 1 1/3 tablespoons unsalted butter

- 1/3 teaspoon salt

- 6 ounces asparagus

- 1/8 teaspoon garlic powder

- 1/3 tablespoon olive oil

- ¼ teaspoon black pepper, ground

Instructions:

1. Turn on the oven, lower the temperature to 400 degrees F and let it warm.

2. Arrange the asparagus on a baking sheet lined with parchment paper, sprinkle with oil, toss

to coat, and bake for 10 minutes, tossing once.

3. Meanwhile, melt the butter in a small bowl by placing it in and heating it for at least 30 seconds on a high heat setting.

4. Once the asparagus is done, pour some butter, sprinkle some yeast, add black pepper, salt, and garlic powder, and toss it all together.

5. Serve immediately.

Nutritional Info: Calories: 108 kcal, Protein: 1.1g, Carb: 3.2g, Fat: 9.8g.

16. Noodles Alfredo with Herby Tofu

(Preparation Time: 10 minutes | Cooking Time: 5 minutes | Serving 4 | Difficulty: Easy)

Ingredients:

- 14 oz. 2 blocks tofu, pressed, extra-firm and cubed

- 1 tbsp mixed herbs, dried

- ¾ cups almond milk, unsweetened

- 4 garlic cloves, roasted (highly recommended, but roasting is optional)

- 1 juiced lemon

- Black pepper and salt to taste

- 2 tbsp vegetable oil

- 12 ounces eggless noodles

- 2 cups cashews, drained and soaked overnight

- ½ cup nutritional yeast

- ½ cup onion, coarsely chopped

- ½ cup tomatoes, sun-dried

- 2 tbsp basil leaves to garnish, chopped fresh

Instructions:

1. Over medium heat, warm your vegetable oil in a big skillet.

2. Tofu is seasoned with mixed herbs, black pepper, and salt before being fried in oil till golden

brown. Transfer to a plate lined with paper towels and reserve. Turn off the heat.

3. Almond milk, garlic, nutritional yeast, lemon juice, and onion should all be combined in a blender. Place aside.

4. Sauté all noodles for two minutes in the vegetable oil reheated in the pan over medium heat. Add your Alfredo sauce, cashew, and sun-dried tomatoes by combining them. Cook the food for two more minutes on low heat.

5. Add more almond milk to the sauce to thin it down if it is too thick.

6. Serve the dish warm after plating and adding the basil garnish.

Nutritional Info: Calories: 268 kcal, Protein: 16g, Carb: 23g, Fat: 12g.

17. Cheesy Potato Casserole

(Preparation Time: 30 minutes | Cooking Time: 20 minutes | Serving 4 | Difficulty: Easy)

Ingredients:

- ½ cup celery stalks, finely chopped

- 1 green bell pepper, finely chopped and seeded

- 2 cups potatoes, chopped and peeled

- 4 oz. vegan Parmesan cheese, freshly shredded

- 2 oz. vegan butter

- 1 white onion, finely chopped

- Black pepper and salt to taste

- 1 cup vegan mayonnaise

- 1 tsp red chili flakes

Instructions:

1. Preheat the oven to 400 F and grease a baking dish with cooking spray.

2. Season the celery, onion, and bell pepper with salt and black pepper.

3. Mix the potatoes, vegan mayonnaise, Parmesan cheese, and red chili flakes in a bowl.

4. Pour the mixture into the baking dish, add the seasoned vegetables, and mix well.

5. Bake in the oven until golden brown, about 20 minutes.

6. Remove the baked potato and serve warm with baby spinach.

Nutritional Info: Calories: 379 kcal, Protein: 21g, Carb: 16g, Fat: 25g.

18. Eggplant Stacks

(Preparation Time: 5 minutes | Cooking Time: 10 minutes | Serving 2 | Difficulty: Easy)

Ingredients:

- ½ teaspoon thyme, dried

- 2 tablespoons olive oil

- ½ pound eggplant

- ½ teaspoon oregano, dried

- 4 tablespoons parmesan cheese, grated

Additional:

- ½ teaspoon black pepper, ground

- ½ teaspoon salt

Instructions:

1. Sliced eggplant should be 1 inch thick. Oil should be brushed on each, and salt, thyme, black pepper, and oregano should be sprinkled on both until well-seasoned.

2. Slices of seasoned eggplant are placed on a hot grill pan, greased with oil and placed over medium heat. The eggplant is then grilled for 3 to 4 minutes on each side or until soft.

3. After that, cover the cheese-topped eggplant slices with a lid and cook them for one to two minutes or until the cheese has melted.

4. Serve immediately.

Nutritional Info: Calories: 200 kcal, Protein: 4.5g, Carb: 7.5g, Fat: 17g.

19. Mushroom Marinated Wraps

(Preparation Time: 15 minutes | Cooking Time: 0 minutes | Serving 2 | Difficulty: Easy)

Ingredients:

- 3 tablespoons lemon juice, fresh

- 2 Portobello mushroom caps, cut into 1-inch strips

- 2 cups baby spinach leaves, fresh

- 1 ripe tomato, chopped

- 3 tablespoons soy sauce

- 1 ½ tablespoons sesame oil, toasted

- 1 ripe Hass avocado, peeled and pitted

- 1 medium red bell pepper, cut into 1-inch strips

- Freshly ground black pepper and salt

Instructions:

1. Combine the oil, 2 tablespoons of lemon juice, and soy sauce in a medium bowl. Portobello strips should then be added, mixed well, and marinated for an hour or overnight. Mushrooms should be drained and placed aside.

2. With the last tablespoon of lemon juice, mash the avocado.

3. Place 1 tortilla on the work surface and top with a portion of the mashed avocado to make wraps. Add a layer of young spinach leaves on top. Place bell pepper strips and a few mushroom strips in the bottom of each tortilla. Add the tomato, salt, and black pepper to your liking. Cut that half diagonally after firmly rolling up.

4. Serve after repeating with the remaining ingredients.

Nutritional Info: Calories: 710 kcal, Protein: 22g, Carb: 53g, Fat: 45g.

20. Scalloped Potatoes

(Preparation Time: 10 minutes | Cooking Time: 30 minutes | Serving 2 | Difficulty: Easy)

Ingredients:

- 3 potatoes, sliced, peeled

- 6 tablespoons unsweetened almond milk

- ¼ teaspoon salt

- 1/3 tablespoon butter, unsalted

- 1 1/3 tablespoon flour

- 2 sliced green onions

- 3 tablespoons parmesan cheese, grated

- ¼ teaspoon black pepper, ground

Instructions:

1. Turn on the oven, lower the temperature to 350 degrees F, and let it warm up.

2. Meanwhile, melt the butter in a small saucepan over low heat. Once it has melted, whisk in the flour until a thick sauce forms. Finally, whisk in the black pepper and salt. After adding the milk and whisking until smooth, turn off the heat and toss in the cheese until it has completely melted.

3. Use some of your potato slices to cover the bottom of a baking pan that has been greased with oil, then top with one-third of the green onions and one-third of the sauce.

4. Using the remaining potatoes, green onion, and sauce, stack two more times, then top with cheese.

5. When the top of the baking pan has gone golden brown, uncover it after 20 minutes and continue baking for another 5 minutes. Serve immediately.

Nutritional Info: Calories: 308 kcal, Protein: 7g, Carb: 57.4g, Fat: 5.4g.

21.   Green Onion and Mushroom Stir-Fry

(Preparation Time: 5 minutes | Cooking Time: 10 minutes | Serving 2 | Difficulty: Easy)

Ingredients:

- 4 ounces mushrooms, sliced
- 1 teaspoon soy sauce
- 1/3 teaspoon salt
- ¼ teaspoon red pepper flakes
- 2 green onions, greens and whites separated, sliced
- ½ teaspoon garlic, minced
- 1 tablespoon olive oil
- ¼ teaspoon black pepper, ground

Instructions:

1. Take a medium skillet, set it at medium heat, add oil, and add half the onion whites when heated. Cook for 2 minutes or until the onions are tender.

2. Stir well after adding the remaining garlic, green onions, and mushrooms, and simmer for 2 to 3 minutes or until the mushrooms are golden brown and soft.

3. Add soy sauce, black pepper, salt, and red pepper flakes. Stir to combine. Cook for an additional minute or until well heated.

4. Serve immediately.

Nutritional Info: Calories: 81 kcal, Protein: 2.7g, Carb: 2.7g, Fat: 6.8g.

22. Chickpeas and Rice

(Preparation Time: 5 minutes | Cooking Time: 15 minutes | Serving 2 | Difficulty: Easy)

Ingredients:

- 6 ounces tinned chickpeas, liquid reserved
- 1 tablespoon olive oil
- 1/3 teaspoon black pepper, ground
- ½ teaspoon cumin seeds

- 1 chopped tomato

- 10 ounces of brown rice

- 2/3 teaspoon salt

- ½ teaspoon red pepper flakes

- Water as required

Instructions:

1. When the oil in the medium skillet is heated, add the tomatoes, swirl, and cook for 2–3 minutes or until the tomatoes are tender.

2. Then swirl to combine and simmer for one minute after adding black pepper, salt, cumin, and red pepper.

3. Add water to the cup of saved chickpea juice to make it 1 2/3 cups full.

4. Add the chickpeas to the pan, toss them until they are evenly coated, cook for one minute, then add the liquid and simmer.

5. Then, add the rice, reduce the heat to medium-low, and simmer for 4 to 5 minutes, or until the rice has absorbed all the water and become soft.

6. When finished, use a fork to fluff the rice before serving.

Nutritional Info: Calories: 709 kcal, Protein: 14.2g, Carb: 133g, Fat: 13.4g.

23. Spinach Casserole

(Preparation Time: 5 minutes | Cooking Time: 10 minutes | Serving 2 | Difficulty: Easy)

Ingredients:

- ¾ tablespoon Italian seasoning

- 3 ounces parmesan cheese, grated

- 1/3 teaspoon salt

- 2 tablespoons olive oil

- 10 ounces spinach

- 1 teaspoon garlic, minced

- 2 tablespoons butter
- ¼ teaspoon black pepper, ground

Instructions:

1. Turn on the oven, lower the temperature to 400 degrees F and let it warm.
2. Cook the spinach for 1 minute, until it has wilted, in a medium saucepan filled halfway with boiling water. Drain the spinach and save it for later use.
3. Heat a small skillet at medium-low heat before adding the butter and oil.
4. When fragrant, whisk in the salt, garlic, and Italian seasoning after which.
5. Take a small casserole dish buttered with butter, pour the butter mixture into it, and then cover it with cheese.
6. Serve the spinach after baking it for about 5 to 8 minutes or until the cheese is melted and well browned.

Nutritional Info: Calories: 435 kcal, Protein: 15.2g, Carb: 10.9g, Fat: 36.7g.

24. Lime Pasta

(Preparation Time: 5 minutes | Cooking Time: 10 minutes | Serving 2 | Difficulty: Easy)

Ingredients:

- 1 tablespoon olive oil
- ¼ teaspoon red pepper flakes
- 1/8 teaspoon black pepper, ground
- 1 lime, zested, juiced
- ¼ teaspoon salt
- 4 ounces of spaghetti

Instructions:

1. Prepare the spaghetti by following the packet's directions for cooking, and then put it aside.
2. Take a small bowl, add lime juice to it, and then mix in the oil, black pepper, salt, and red pepper flakes.

3. Place the cooked pasta on two dishes, top with all the lime mixture in a uniform layer, and toss to combine.

4. Serve immediately.

Nutritional Info: Calories: 210 kcal, Protein: 5.1g, Carb: 29.1g, Fat: 7.5g.

25. *Zucchini Meatballs*

(Preparation Time: 20 minutes | Cooking Time: 25 minutes | Serving 4 | Difficulty: Moderate)

Ingredients:

- 3 garlic cloves
- 1 teaspoon of basil, dried
- ½ teaspoon of salt
- juice of ½ lemon
- 32 ounces of marinara
- 15-ounces 1 tin of chickpeas, rinsed and drained
- ½ cup of rolled oats
- 1 teaspoon of oregano, dried
- 2 tablespoons of nutritional yeast
- 1 cup of shredded zucchini (almost 1 large zucchini)
- 8 ounces of whole grain pasta

Instructions:

1. Combine the chickpeas, rolled oats, and garlic cloves rinsed and dried in the food processor's bowl. Wait until the food is well chopped and pulse for 5 to 10 seconds. The mixture should hold together when you press your fingers together. Transfer it to a large bowl with lemon juice, dried herbs, salt, nutritional yeast, and shredded zucchini. Make sure you use one cup of zucchini that has been shredded.

2. Stir them until they are well mixed. If the mixture is too moist to handle, just a little flour should be added. Extra nuts may be ground into flour or nutritional yeast. This flour will help to absorb more moisture when added.

3. The oven should be heated to 375°F. Then line a baking sheet with parchment paper. One heaping spoonful of the zucchini mixture at a time, scoop out and roll with your hands into 12 individual balls. Place a few inches apart on the baking sheet, then bake for approximately 25 minutes. Meanwhile, prepare the pasta as directed.

4. When the zucchini balls become a light golden brown, remove them from the oven and set them aside. Serve the warm pasta with marinara sauce and top with fresh basil.

Nutritional Info: Calories: 259 kcal, Protein: 10g, Carb: 30g, Fat: 12g.

26. The Tempeh Chili

(Preparation Time: 5 minutes | Cooking Time: 25 minutes | Serving 4 | Difficulty: Easy)

Ingredients:

- 226g or 8 ounces 1 package tempeh, roughly grated

- 1 diced red bell pepper

- 2 minced garlic cloves

- 15 ounces or 425 g 1 tin kidney beans, drained

- 1 cup or 24ml of water

- ¼ teaspoon chili powder

- ¼ teaspoon red pepper flakes, crushed

- Plain Greek yogurt (optional)

- 30ml or 2 tablespoons of olive oil

- 1 medium white onion, diced

- 1 stalk celery, diced

- ¾ cup or 177ml of tomato sauce

- 1 15 ounces or 425 g tin of black beans, drained

- 1 teaspoon of each salt and cumin

- Green onions, chopped (optional)

Instructions:

1. Inside a big saucepan, heat the oil over medium to high heat. Mix the tempeh, and cook for approximately five minutes or once it is faintly browned. It's OK if part of it sinks to the base of the pan. It will fall off once the liquids are added.

2. Add flavor producers: Combine celery, onion, bell pepper, and garlic; cook for 5 minutes or until the vegetables are somewhat tender.

3. Preparing Everything: Add the other ingredients, reduce the heat to medium, and cook for approximately 15 minutes or until the mixture is warm. Taste and adjust the meal if you'd like. Top with green onions.

Nutritional Info: Calories: 426 kcal, Protein: 33g, Carb: 56g, Fat: 11g.

27. Mushroom Patties and Herbs

(Preparation Time: 10 minutes | Cooking Time: 20 minutes | Serving 15 patties | Difficulty: Easy)

Ingredients:

- 5 tbsps. hemp seeds
- 1 onion, chopped
- 2 tbsps. flax seeds, ground
- 4 tbsps. nutritional yeast
- 4 tbsps. white wine (optional)
- 1 tbsp oil for cooking
- 4 cups of button mushrooms, chopped
- 3 tbsps. dill, chopped
- 2 tbsps. dry thyme
- 1 large egg or 3 tablespoons water
- 3 to 4 tbsps. hemp protein powder
- 3 tbsps. oil for baking or frying
- Black pepper and sea salt, ground for taste

Instructions:

1. Mix the ground flax and water in a small dish, and then let it thicken for five minutes.

2. 1 tablespoon of oil should be heated in a big skillet before adding chopped onion and sautéing for around two minutes.

3. Wine, salt, chopped mushrooms, dry thyme, and pepper should all be combined. Sauté for ten minutes, then cover with a lid.

4. Refrain from heat.

5. Add the egg or flax egg, and active dry yeast flakes. Now combine all the ingredients.

6. Hemp seeds, chopped dill, and hemp protein powder, should be combined. When adding hemp protein powder, mix 3 tablespoons at a time. You cannot produce the patties as easily if the composition is too high. Therefore you must add more until it has the proper consistency. The hemp powder will absorb all surplus water.

Nutritional Info: Calories: 259 kcal, Protein: 8.6g, Carb: 45g, Fat: 4.1g.

28. Stuffed peppers

(Preparation Time: 40 minutes | Cooking Time: 15 minutes | Serving 8 | Difficulty: Easy)

Ingredients:

- 2 cups tofu, crumbled, pressed
- ½ cup cilantro, freshly chopped
- ¼ cup lime juice
- ½ teaspoon salt
- 8 large bell peppers, deseeded, halved lengthwise
- 15 ounces each 2 tins of black beans, rinsed, drained
- ¾ cup green onions, thinly sliced
- ¼ cup vegetable oil
- 3 cloves garlic, finely chopped
- ½ teaspoon chili powder
- 3 Roma tomatoes, diced

Instructions:

1. To create the filling, combine all the ingredients in a dish except the bell peppers.

2. This mixture is put into the peppers.

3. Cut eight foils with a dimension of 18 into 12 inches, each sheet of aluminum foil with two halves. Leave a space on the sides when you seal the peppers.

4. Grill for around 15 minutes over direct heat.

5. Add some cilantro, and then serve.

Nutritional Info: Calories: 379 kcal, Protein: 21g, Carb: 16g, Fat: 25g.

Chapter 6: Smoothies & Drinks

Below are the recipes.

1. Banana and Spinach Smoothie

(Preparation Time: 5 minutes | Cooking Time: 0 minutes | Serving 2 | Difficulty: Easy)

Ingredients:

- 4 ounces spinach

- 1 cup unsweetened almond milk

- 2 peeled bananas

- 2 tablespoons almond butter

- ½ cup water

Additional:

- ½ cup of ice cubes

Instructions:

1. In a blender or food processor, combine all the ingredients in the specified order and pulse for 1 to 2 minutes or until smooth.

2. The blender should be divided between two glasses before being served.

Nutritional Info: Calories: 248 kcal, Protein: 5.6g, Carb: 34.1g, Fat: 9.9g.

2. Fruity Smoothie

(Preparation Time: 10 minutes | Cooking Time: 0 minutes | Serving 1 | Difficulty: Easy)

Ingredients:

- ½ cup pineapple juice
- 1 cup sliced raspberries
- ¾ cup soy yogurt
- 1 cup pineapple chunks
- 1 cup sliced blueberries

Instructions:

1. Blend all ingredients inside a food processor.
2. Before serving, chill.

Nutritional Info: Calories: 279 kcal, Protein: 12g, Carb: 56g, Fat: 2g.

3. Mango Smoothie

(Preparation Time: 5 minutes | Cooking Time: 0 minutes | Serving 3 | Difficulty: Easy)

Ingredients:

- 1 cup strawberries
- 1 cup chopped peaches
- 1 cup chopped mango
- 1 carrot, chopped and peeled
- 1 cup water
- 1 banana, sliced and frozen

Instructions:

1. Blend all ingredients inside a food processor.
2. Before serving, chill.

Nutritional Info: Calories: 376 kcal, Protein: 5g, Carb: 95g, Fat: 2g.

4. Spiced Warm Lemon Drink

(Preparation Time: 10 minutes | Cooking Time: 2 hours | Serving 12 | Difficulty: Hard)

Ingredients:

- ½ teaspoon of whole cloves

- 4 fluids of ounce pineapple juice

- 12 fluid ounces of orange juice

- 1 cinnamon stick, around 3 inches long

- 2 cups of coconut sugar

- ½ cup and 2 tablespoons of lemon juice

- 2 ½ quarts of water

Instructions:

1. Fill a 6-quart slow cooker with water and thoroughly whisk in the lemon juice and sugar.

2. Whole cloves and cinnamon should be wrapped in cheesecloth with the corners secured with thread.

3. Place the lid on the slow cooker and place this cheesecloth bag within the liquid.

4. Then turn on the slow cooker and allow it to stew for two hours on high heat or until it is well cooked.

5. Once finished, remove your cheesecloth bag and serve the warm or chilled beverage.

Nutritional Info: Calories: 15 kcal, Protein: 0.1g, Carb: 3.2g, Fat: 0g.

5. Warm Pomegranate Punch

(Preparation Time: 15 minutes | Cooking Time: 3 hours | Serving 10 | Difficulty: Hard)

Ingredients:

- 12 whole cloves

- 1/3 cup of lemon juice

- 32 fluid ounces of apple juice, unsweetened

- 3 cinnamon sticks, around 3 inches long each

- ½ cup of coconut sugar

- 32 fluid ounces of pomegranate juice

- 16 fluid ounces of brewed tea

Instructions:

1. Pour the lemon juice, apple juice, pomegranate juice, sugar, and tea, into a 4-quart slow cooker.

2. The entire cinnamon stick and cloves should be placed in the liquid in the slow cooker after being wrapped with cheesecloth and tied at the corners with twine.

3. Then put the lid on it, turn the slow cooker on to the low heat setting, and cook it for three hours, or until it is well cooked.

4. Once finished, remove your cheesecloth bag and serve the dish warm or cold.

Nutritional Info: Calories: 253 kcal, Protein: 7g, Carb: 58g, Fat: 2g.

6. Nice Spiced Cherry Cider

(Preparation Time: 5 minutes | Cooking Time: 4 hours | Serving 16 | Difficulty: Easy)

Ingredients:

- 6-ounce of cherry gelatin

- 2 cinnamon sticks, around 3 inches long each

- 4 quarts of apple cider

Instructions:

1. Pour the apple cider into a 6-quart slow cooker, and then add your cinnamon stick.

2. Stir, and then put the lid on the slow cooker. Connect the cooker to the outlet and leave it on high heat for 3 hours or once properly heated.

3. After correctly adding and stirring the gelatin, simmer the mixture for another hour.

4. Once finished, remove all cinnamon sticks and serve the beverage warm or chilled.

Nutritional Info: Calories: 100 kcal, Protein: 0g, Carb: 0g, Fat: 0g.

7. Energizing Detox Ginger Tonic

(Preparation Time: 15 minutes | Cooking Time: 10 minutes | Serving 2 | Difficulty: Easy)

Ingredients:

- 1 small lemon slice

- 1/8 teaspoon of turmeric, ground

- 1 teaspoon of maple syrup

- 2 cups of boiling water

- ½ teaspoon of ginger, fresh grated

- 1/8 teaspoon of cayenne pepper

- 1/8 teaspoon of cinnamon, ground

- 1 teaspoon of apple cider vinegar

Instructions:

1. The ginger should be added to a small saucepan with boiling water, stirred, and rest for about eight to ten minutes before covering the pan.

2. Add the cayenne, cinnamon, and turmeric to the liquid. After straining the mixture, stir well.

3. Add the lemon slice, vinegar, and maple syrup.

4. Serve right away after adding and stirring one flavored lemon.

Nutritional Info: Calories: 80 kcal, Protein: 0g, Carb: 0g, Fat: 0g.

8. Ultimate Mulled Wine

(Preparation Time: 5 minutes | Cooking Time: 30 minutes | Serving 6 | Difficulty: Easy)

Ingredients:

- 2 juiced oranges

- 2 cinnamon sticks, around 3 inches long each

- 1/3 cup of honey

- 8 fluid ounces of cranberry juice

- 1 cup of cranberries, fresh

- 1 tablespoon of whole cloves

- 1 tablespoon of star anise

- 8 fluid ounces of apple cider

- 24 fluid ounces of red wine

Instructions:

1. Add each item to a 4-quart slow cooker and give everything a good stir.

2. Cook it for about 30 minutes on high heat or until it is well warmed, with the lid on and the slow cooker plugged in.

3. When finished, immediately serve the wine after straining.

Nutritional Info: Calories: 202 kcal, Protein: 0g, Carb: 25g, Fat: 0g.

9. Soothing Tea Drink

(Preparation Time: 5 minutes | Cooking Time: 2 hours 10 minutes | Serving 8 | Difficulty: Easy)

Ingredients:

- 2 tablespoons of honey

- 32 fluid ounces of white grape juice

- 1 tablespoon ginger root, minced

- 15 green tea bags

- 2 quarts of boiling water

Instructions:

1. Tea bags should be submerged in water in a 4-quart slow cooker before the pot is covered and left to stand for about 10 minutes.

2. Remove and discard the tea bags after ten minutes, then whisk in the other ingredients.

3. Put the slow cooker's lid back on; plug it in and set the heat to high for two hours or until everything has cooked through.

4. Once finished, drain the liquid, then serve warm or cold.

Nutritional Info: Calories: 45 kcal, Protein: 0g, Carb: 12g, Fat: 0g.

10. Pleasant Lemonade

(Preparation Time: 15 minutes | Cooking Time: 3 hours | Serving 10 | Difficulty: Moderate)

Ingredients:

- 2 cups of coconut sugar

- 3 cups of lemon juice. fresh

- Cinnamon sticks for serving

- ¼ cup of honey

- 32 fluid ounces of water

Instructions:

1. Place all your ingredients in a 4-quart slow cooker, excluding the cinnamon sticks, and mix well.

2. Put the cover on it, turn the slow cooker on to the low heat setting, and cook it for three hours or until it is well cooked.

3. Once finished, stir everything well and serve using the cinnamon sticks.

Nutritional Info: Calories: 146 kcal, Protein: 0g, Carb: 34g, Fat: 0g.

11. Fragrant Spiced Coffee

(Preparation Time: 10 minutes | Cooking Time: 3 hours | Serving 8 | Difficulty: Easy)

Ingredients:

- 1 ½ teaspoons of whole cloves

- 2-ounce of chocolate syrup

- 8 cups of brewed coffee

- 4 cinnamon sticks, around 3 inches long each

- 1/3 cup of honey

- ½ teaspoon of anise extract

Instructions:

1. In a 4-quart slow cooker, add the coffee. Add the other ingredients, except the cinnamon,

and mix well.

2. Cloves should be wrapped entirely in cheesecloth, with the corners secured with threads.

3. Place the lid on the slow cooker and place this cheesecloth bag within the liquid.

4. After that, turn on the slow cooker and allow it to stew for three hours on low heat or until well cooked.

5. Serve after removing the cheesecloth bag.

Nutritional Info: Calories: 150 kcal, Protein: 3g, Carb: 35g, Fat: 0g.

12. Rich Truffle Hot Chocolate

(Preparation Time: 10 minutes | Cooking Time: 2 hours | Serving 4 | Difficulty: Easy)

Ingredients:

- 1/3 cup of coconut sugar

- 1/8 teaspoon cinnamon, ground

- 32 fluid ounces of coconut milk

- 1/3 cup of unsweetened cocoa powder

- 1/8 teaspoon of salt

- 1 teaspoon of unsweetened vanilla extract

Instructions:

1. Add each item to a 2-quart slow cooker and give everything a good stir.

2. Cook it for about 2 hours on high heat, or until well cooked, with the cover on and the slow cooker plugged in.

3. When finished, immediately serve.

Nutritional Info: Calories: 67 kcal, Protein: 2g, Carb: 13g, Fat: 2g.

Chapter 7: Snacks & Desserts

Below are the recipes.

1. Asparagus and Chickpeas Salad

(Preparation Time: 10 minutes | Cooking Time: 10 minutes | Serving 2 | Difficulty: Easy)

Ingredients:

- 6 ounces tin of chickpeas, liquid reserved
- 1 sliced green onion
- 7 ounces potato, diced
- 6 ounces asparagus
- 1 ¼ tablespoon balsamic vinegar

Additional:

- 1 ¼ tablespoon water
- 1/8 teaspoon basil, dried
- ½ teaspoon salt
- 1/8 teaspoon garlic powder
- 1/3 tablespoon lime juice

Instructions:

1. Turn on the oven, lower the temperature to 425 degrees F and let it warm up.
2. Meanwhile, put the potatoes in a medium saucepan, add water to cover, and simmer for 5 to 7 minutes on medium heat.
3. Meanwhile, put asparagus on a baking sheet that has been greased with oil.
4. Add garlic powder and onions to the top, and then roast for 8 minutes, stirring halfway through.
5. Combine the lime juice, vinegar, and water in a small bowl to make the dressing. Stir in the salt and basil until well combined.
6. Once the potatoes are cooked, drain them, place them in a medium bowl, and stir in the

chickpeas.

7. Add the asparagus, sprinkle the salad dressing as directed, toss to combine, and serve.

Nutritional Info: Calories: 211 kcal, Protein: 8g, Carb: 9.2g, Fat: 2.3g.

2. Nori Snack Rolls

(Preparation Time: 5 minutes | Cooking Time: 10 minutes | Serving 4 rolls | Difficulty: Easy)

Ingredients:

- 2 tablespoons soy sauce or tamari

- 1 sliced mushroom

- ½ cup carrots, grated

- 2 tablespoons almond, peanut, cashew, or other nut butter

- 4 standard nori sheets

- 1 tablespoon pickled ginger

Instructions:

1. Set the oven to 350 degrees Fahrenheit.

2. Tamari and nut butter should be combined well until extremely thick.

3. A nori sheet should be laid out the long way, rough side up.

4. Run a thin line of your tamari mixture from side to side on the other end of the nori sheet. On the other side, the one closest to you, arrange the carrots, ginger, and mushroom slices in a line.

5. When rolling toward your tahini mixture, fold the veggies within the nori to close the roll. To create four rolls, repeat.

6. The rolls should be slightly browned and crispy at the ends after 8 to 10 minutes in the oven. Slice each roll into three smaller pieces after letting them cool for a few minutes.

Nutritional Info: Calories: 79 kcal, Protein: 4g, Carb: 6g, Fat: 5g.

3. Avocado Toast with Flaxseeds

(Preparation Time: 5 minutes | Cooking Time: 0 minutes | Serving 3 | Difficulty: Easy)

Ingredients:

- 1 avocado, large ripe
- 1 tbsp. flax seeds
- 1 tbsp. lime juice
- 3 slices of bread, whole grain
- ¼ cup parsley, chopped
- 1 tbsp. sesame seeds

Instructions:

1. Toast your slice of bread first.
2. Get rid of the avocado seed.
3. Half an avocado should be cut and mashed with a fork in a bowl.
4. On two pieces of toast, spread mashed avocado.
5. One toast with one avocado slices on it.
6. Add sesame and flax seeds on top.
7. Sprinkle freshly cut parsley and lime juice over the top.
8. Dispense and savor!

Nutritional Info: Calories: 379 kcal, Protein: 31g, Carb: 98g, Fat: 124g.

4. Cinnamon Oranges

(Preparation Time: 5 minutes | Cooking Time: 0 minutes | Serving 2 | Difficulty: Easy)

Ingredients:

- ½ tablespoon coconut sugar
- 1 tablespoon orange juice
- 2 oranges

- ¼ teaspoon cinnamon, ground

- 1 tablespoon lime juice

Instructions:

1. To prepare the oranges, cut each into six slices after removing the white pith and peel.

2. In a small dish, combine the juices of the orange and lime. Once the sugar has fully dissolved, add the cinnamon.

3. Oranges should be distributed among plates before the cinnamon mixture is drizzled over them.

Nutritional Info: Calories: 99.5 kcal, Protein: 1.5g, Carb: 23g, Fat: 0.2g.

5. Plant-Based Crispy Falafel

(Preparation Time: 20 minutes | Cooking Time: 30 minutes | Serving 8 | Difficulty: Easy)

Ingredients:

- 1 cup chickpeas, dried and soaked inside the refrigerator for 24 hours

- ½ cup chopped red onion

- 2 cloves garlic, quartered

- ½ tsp. Black pepper ground

- ¼ tsp. cinnamon, ground

- 1 tbsp. olive oil, extra-virgin

- 1 cup chopped cauliflower

- ½ cup packed parsley, fresh

- 1 tsp. sea salt

- ½ tsp. cumin, ground

Instructions:

1. Bake at 375 degrees Fahrenheit.

2. Chickpeas, onion, cauliflower, parsley, salt, garlic, pepper, cinnamon, cumin seeds, and olive oil should all be combined in a food processor until the mixture is smooth.

3. Make two tablespoons worth of the mixture into little patties for the falafel.

4. Maintain falafel on an oiled baking sheet.

5. Falafel should be baked in a preheated oven for 25 to 30 minutes or until golden brown on both sides.

6. Remove cooked food from the oven.

7. Enjoy a hot, fresh veggie salad!

Nutritional Info: Calories: 322 kcal, Protein: 19g, Carb: 71g, Fat: 29g.

6. Spinach and Strawberry Salad

(Preparation Time: 5 minutes | Cooking Time: 0 minutes | Serving 2 | Difficulty: Easy)

Ingredients:

- 4 ounces sliced strawberry

- 1/3 cup slivered almonds

- 6 ounces of spinach leaves

- ½ of avocado, pitted, peeled, and sliced

- 4 tablespoons olive oil

Additional:

- ¼ teaspoon salt

- 2 tablespoons balsamic vinegar

- ¼ teaspoon garlic powder

- ½ teaspoon maple syrup

- ½ tablespoon mustard paste

Instructions:

1. Prepare the dressing by placing the oil, salt, vinegar, mustard, and maple syrup in a small bowl and whisking until emulsified.

2. Place strawberries, avocado, and spinach on two plates, top with prepared dressing, and then serve.

Nutritional Info: Calories: 349 kcal, Protein: 2.6g, Carb: 11.3g, Fat: 32.4g.

7. Fried Avocados

(Preparation Time: 10 minutes | Cooking Time: 6 minutes | Serving 2 | Difficulty: Easy)

Ingredients:

- 1 teaspoon paprika
- 1 ½ tablespoon olive oil
- 1 avocado, pitted, peeled
- ¾ teaspoon salt

Instructions:

1. Cut the avocado in half lengthwise, remove the pit, peel it, and then season with paprika and salt to finish preparing it.
2. Oil should be added to a medium skillet pan, which should be heated up over medium heat.
3. After that, add seasoned avocados and toast them for 3 minutes on each side.
4. Avocados should be sliced into slices after cooling for 5 minutes.
5. Serve immediately.

Nutritional Info: Calories: 203 kcal, Protein: 1.5g, Carb: 5.1g, Fat: 19.6g.

8. Apple Cinnamon Skillet

(Preparation Time: 5 minutes | Cooking Time: 10 minutes | Serving 2 | Difficulty: Easy)

Ingredients:

- ½ tablespoon coconut oil
- ½ teaspoon cornstarch
- ½ teaspoon cinnamon
- 2 apples, cored, peeled, sliced
- 1 ½ tablespoon coconut sugar
- ¼ cup of cold water

- ½ teaspoon vanilla extract, unsweetened

Instructions:

1. A medium frying pan should be used. Heat it at medium heat, add the oil, and wait for it to melt, then add the apple slices and cook for three minutes.

2. Take a little bowl, add the cornstarch, add the water, swirl to combine, and save until needed.

3. When the apple slices are fork soft, sprinkle the cornstarch mixture over them and add vanilla, sugar, and cinnamon. Stir to blend, and then bring to a moderate boil for 2 minutes.

4. Take the skillet from the heat, give the apple five minutes to cool, and serve.

Nutritional Info: Calories: 226 kcal, Protein: 0g, Carb: 47.6g, Fat: 4g.

9. Baked Potato

(Preparation Time: 5 minutes | Cooking Time: 12 minutes | Serving 2 | Difficulty: Easy)

Ingredients:

- ½ teaspoon salt

- 2 tablespoons olive oil

- 2 red potatoes, medium

- ¼ teaspoon black pepper, ground

Instructions:

1. Turn on the oven, lower the temperature to 450 degrees F and let it warm.

2. After washing, split the potatoes in half.

3. Put the potato on a baking sheet, line it using parchment paper, and then coat it with oil.

4. Potatoes should be salted and peppered before being turned cut-side up and pricked with a fork.

5. Potatoes should be baked for ten to twelve minutes until they are tender and the edges are golden. After 5 minutes, serve.

Nutritional Info: Calories: 264 kcal, Protein: 2.6g, Carb: 33.6g, Fat: 13.2g.

10. Whole Wheat Chocolate Waffle

(Preparation Time: 5 minutes | Cooking Time: 5 minutes | Serving 2 | Difficulty: Easy)

Ingredients:

- 2 tablespoons cocoa powder
- 1 tablespoon olive oil
- ¼ teaspoon vanilla extract, unsweetened
- ½ cup flour, whole-wheat
- ½ teaspoon baking powder
- ½ cup almond milk, unsweetened
- 2 tablespoons coconut sugar

Instructions:

1. To warm up, a tiny waffle maker should be turned on for five minutes.
2. Meanwhile, combine all the ingredients in a medium bowl and blend with an immersion blender once smooth.
3. Pour the batter into the waffle machine in a uniform layer, cover it, and cook it for 3 to 4 minutes until golden brown and firm.
4. Serve immediately.

Nutritional Info: Calories: 185 kcal, Protein: 4.1g, Carb: 22.5g, Fat: 8.6g.

11. Balsamic Avocado

(Preparation Time: 5 minutes | Cooking Time: 0 minutes | Serving 2 | Difficulty: Easy)

Ingredients:

- 2 tablespoons balsamic vinegar
- 2 teaspoons lime juice
- 1 avocado
- 1 teaspoon olive oil

Instructions:

1. Cut the avocado in lengthwise half, peel it, and then remove the pit to prepare it.

2. Olive oil should be drizzled after the vinegar and lime juices have been added to the avocado.

3. Serve immediately.

Nutritional Info: Calories: 153 kcal, Protein: 1.5g, Carb: 9.5g, Fat: 12g.

12. Strawberry Blender Pancakes

(Preparation Time: 5 minutes | Cooking Time: 10 minutes | Serving 2 | Difficulty: Easy)

Ingredients:

- 4 tablespoons peanut butter

- 2 ounces strawberries

- 1/8 teaspoon cinnamon

- ½ cup almond milk, unsweetened

- 1 peeled banana

- ¼ cup flour, whole-wheat

- 1 tablespoon maple syrup

- 1 tablespoon olive oil

Instructions:

1. Except for the oil, combine all the ingredients in a blender. Pulse for 2 minutes or until smooth.

2. Take the medium skillet pan, pour oil, and heat it until hot.

3. Fill the pan with batter, shape the batter into pancakes, and cook the pancakes for 2 to 3 minutes on each side or once done and golden brown.

4. Repeat the process with the remaining batter after transferring the cooked pancakes to a platter.

5. Serve immediately.

Nutritional Info: Calories: 405 kcal, Protein: 9g, Carb: 39g, Fat: 23.1g.

13. Orange Parfait

(Preparation Time: 10 minutes | Cooking Time: 10 minutes | Serving 2 | Difficulty: Easy)

Ingredients:

- 3 tablespoons chia seeds

- 3 tablespoon maple syrup

- ½ teaspoon unsweetened vanilla extract

- 2 oranges

- 2 ½ tablespoons coconut, shredded unsweetened

- 6 ounces of unsweetened almond milk

Instructions:

1. Chia and coconut should be blended with maple syrup, milk, and vanilla in a medium bowl. Chia and coconut should also be combined with chia and coconut.

2. After allowing the mixture to sit for 30 minutes, whisk it and chill it for at least 3 hours or overnight.

3. When ready to dine, peel all oranges, cut each into eight slices, and discard the white pith.

4. When the grill pan is hot, add the orange slices and cook for 4 to 5 minutes on each side until light brown.

5. Build the parfait by putting four orange slices in the bottom of each serving glass, followed by half of your chia mixture.

6. The remaining orange slices are on top of the chia layer and then top with the leftover chia mixture before serving immediately.

Nutritional Info: Calories: 210 kcal, Protein: 3.1g, Carb: 28g, Fat: 8.8g.

14. Caramelize Oven-baked Plantains

(Preparation Time: 30 minutes | Cooking Time: 17 minutes | Serving 4 | Difficulty: Moderate)

Ingredients:

- 2 tbsp orange juice, fresh

- 1 tbsp orange zest, grated

- 4 medium plantains, sliced and peeled

- 4 tbsp brown sugar or more for taste

- 4 tbsp coconut butter, melted

Instructions:

1. Set the oven to 180 C or 360 F.

2. Put slices of plantain inside a heatproof dish.

3. Plantains should be covered with orange juice before being dusted with orange zest and brown sugar.

4. Plantains should be coated evenly in melted coconut butter.

5. For 15 to 17 minutes, bake with a foil cover.

6. Serve with maple syrup or honey, warm or cold.

Nutritional Info: Calories: 135 kcal, Protein: 11g, Carb: 6g, Fat: 2g.

15. Sweet Truffles

(Preparation Time: 5 minutes | Cooking Time: 0 minutes | Serving 2 | Difficulty: Easy)

Ingredients:

- ¾ cup pecans

- ½ teaspoon cinnamon, ground

- 2 tablespoons coconut, shredded

- ½ cup Medjool dates, chopped, pitted

- ¼ teaspoon vanilla extract, unsweetened

Instructions:

1. Add all the ingredients (apart from the coconut) to a food processor and pulse for one or

more minutes until incorporated.

2. Make six balls of the mixture, and then roll them inside the coconut.

3. Serve immediately.

Nutritional Info: Calories: 475 kcal, Protein: 4.7g, Carb: 45g, Fat: 30.5g.

16. Carrot Fritters

(Preparation Time: 5 minutes | Cooking Time: 6 minutes | Serving 2 | Difficulty: Easy)

Ingredients:

- 1 cup carrot, grated
- ½ tablespoon garlic, minced
- ½ teaspoon salt
- 1/3 teaspoon cumin
- 1 tablespoon olive oil
- 2 tablespoons flour
- 2 green onion, sliced
- ¼ cup of water
- ¼ teaspoon black pepper, ground
- 1/3 teaspoon paprika

Instructions:

1. Combine the flour, black pepper, salt, paprika, and cumin in a medium bowl. Stir in the water until the mixture is smooth.

2. After letting the mixture sit for 15 minutes, whisk in the carrot and green onions.

3. Put a medium skillet at medium heat, add the oil, and when it's hot, add spoonfuls of the batter made.

4. The batter should be shaped into pancakes, fried, and properly browned on each side for two to three minutes.

5. Serve immediately.

Nutritional Info: Calories: 123 kcal, Protein: 1.2g, Carb: 13.6g, Fat: 7g.

Chapter 8: Soups & Stews

Below are the recipes.

1. Green Onion Soup

(Preparation Time: 5 minutes | Cooking Time: 12 minutes | Serving 2 | Difficulty: Easy)

Ingredients:

- 7 ounces potatoes, diced
- 2 tablespoons olive oil
- 6 chopped green onions
- 1/3 teaspoon salt
- 1 ¼ cup vegetable broth

Additional:

- ¼ teaspoon coriander, ground
- ¼ teaspoon white pepper, ground

Instructions:

1. Place the potato in a small pan, add the water, and then heat the pan at medium heat.
2. When the potato is cooked and soft, drain your potatoes and save them for later use.
3. Once the oil is heated, add the green onions and simmer for five minutes on low heat.
4. Add potatoes, season with pepper, salt, and coriander, then pour in the vegetable stock, mix well, and boil.
5. After that, turn off the heat and use an immersion blender to puree the mixture until it is creamy.
6. Ladle the soup into dishes after tasting it to check the seasoning.
7. The soup should be chilled before being divided equally among two meal prep boxes, sealed with a lid, and kept in the fridge for up to 7 days. The soup should be heated in the microwave for one to two minutes when it's time to eat.

Nutritional Info: Calories: 191 kcal, Protein: 1.9g, Carb: 1.9g, Fat: 13.6g.

2. Roasted Creamy Beet Soup

(Preparation Time: 10 minutes | Cooking Time: 1 hour 15 minutes | Serving 4 | Difficulty: Easy)

Ingredients:

- 1-pound beets, scrubbed and trimmed

- 1 teaspoon garlic, chopped

- ¼ teaspoon dill, dried

- 1 bay laurel

- Ground black pepper and sea salt

- 1 tablespoon red wine vinegar

- 2 tablespoons olive oil

- 1 red onion, large chopped

- ¼ teaspoon cumin, ground

- ½ teaspoon oregano, dried

- 4 cups vegetable broth

- 1 teaspoon red pepper flakes

- 1 cup coconut milk, full-fat

Instructions:

1. Start by setting the oven to 400 degrees Fahrenheit. Wrap the beets loosely in aluminum foil and toss with one tablespoon of olive oil.

2. Check the beets after 20 minutes and roast them for approximately an hour. The roasted beets should be divided into wedges and placed aside.

3. Meanwhile, heat the last tablespoon of olive oil in a heavy-bottomed saucepan at medium to high heat. Now, sauté your onion for 4 minutes or until it becomes translucent and soft.

4. Garlic, dill, cumin, bay leaf, and oregano should be added, and sautéing should continue for 1 minute or until aromatic.

5. After stirring in the salt, vegetable broth, black pepper, roasted beets, and red pepper

flakes, bring it to a rolling boil. Instantaneously lower the heat to boil and allow the food to cook for 20 to 22 minutes.

6. Using an immersion blender, puree the soup until it is smooth and creamy.

7. Put the blended mixture back in the saucepan. When fully cooked, simmer for another 5 minutes while incorporating the coconut milk.

8. Serve hot and ladle into separate bowls.

Nutritional Info: Calories: 308 kcal, Protein: 8.8g, Carb: 20.2g, Fat: 22.8g.

3. Winter Bean Soup

(Preparation Time: 10 minutes | Cooking Time: 20 minutes | Serving 4 | Difficulty: Easy)

Ingredients:

- 2 tablespoons chopped shallots
- 1 chopped parsnip
- 1 teaspoon garlic, fresh minced
- 2 bay leaves
- 16 ounces tin of navy beans
- 1 tablespoon olive oil
- 1 chopped carrot
- 1 chopped celery stalk
- 4 cups vegetable broth
- 1 chopped rosemary sprig
- Ground black pepper and flaky sea salt to taste

Instructions:

1. The olive should be heated over medium-high heat in a heavy-bottomed saucepan. Now, sauté the celery, shallots, carrot, and parsnip for about 3 minutes or until the veggies soften.

2. When the garlic is fragrant, add it and mix to sauté for 1 minute.

3. Bring to a boil after adding the vegetable broth, rosemary, and bay leaves.

4. Lower the heat to boil as soon as possible and allow the food to cook for 10 minutes.

5. After adding the navy beans, boil the mixture for 5 minutes to ensure that everything is properly heated. To taste, add black pepper and salt to the food.

6. Discard all bay leaves after ladling them into separate bowls and serving hot.

Nutritional Info: Calories: 234 kcal, Protein: 14.4g, Carb: 32.3g, Fat: 5.5g.

4. Cucumber and Avocado Soup

(Preparation Time: 5 minutes | Cooking Time: 0 minutes | Serving 2 | Difficulty: Easy)

Ingredients:

- 1 chopped cucumber
- ½ teaspoon garlic powder
- 1 medium avocado, pitted, peeled, and sliced
- ¼ of a lime juiced
- ½ cup water

Additional:

- 1 teaspoon cumin, ground
- ¼ teaspoon salt

Instructions:

1. Put all your ingredients in a food processor and process for two to three minutes or until the mixture is smooth.

2. Place the soup inside the refrigerator for about 45 minutes, divide it into two bowls and serve.

Nutritional Info: Calories: 139 kcal, Protein: 1.7g, Carb: 10.7g, Fat: 9.8g.

5. Potato Soup

(Preparation Time: 5 minutes | Cooking Time: 12 minutes | Serving 2 | Difficulty: Easy)

Ingredients:

- 1/3 teaspoon salt

- 1 ½ cup vegetable broth

- 2 potatoes, cubed and peeled

- 4 teaspoons parmesan cheese, grated

- ¾ cup of water

Additional:

- 1 tablespoon Cajun seasoning

- 1/8 teaspoon black pepper, ground

Instructions:

1. Potato cubes are placed in a small pan, filled with vegetable broth and water and heated over medium heat.

2. Once the potato is cooked and soft, take it from the heat and use an immersion blender to puree the mixture until it is smooth.

3. Reset the heat to medium-low, add the other ingredients, whisk to combine, and then simmer the mixture.

4. Ladle the soup into dishes after tasting it to check the seasoning.

5. The soup should be chilled before being divided equally among two meal prep boxes, sealed with a lid, and kept in the fridge for up to 7 days. The soup should be heated in the microwave for one to two minutes when it's time to eat.

Nutritional Info: Calories: 210 kcal, Protein: 6.8g, Carb: 37g, Fat: 3.7g.

6. Amaranth Vegetable Soup

(Preparation Time: 10 minutes | Cooking Time: 25 minutes | Serving 4 | Difficulty: Easy)

Ingredients:

- 1 shallot, small chopped

- 1 parsnip, chopped and trimmed

- 1 teaspoon fennel seeds

- 1 teaspoon turmeric powder

- ½ cup amaranth

- 2 cups water

- Ground black pepper and sea salt, for taste

- 2 tablespoons olive oil

- 1 carrot, chopped and trimmed

- 1 cup yellow squash, chopped and peeled

- 1 teaspoon celery seeds

- 1 bay laurel

- 2 cups cream of celery soup

- 2 cups collard greens, torn into pieces

Instructions:

1. Warm up the olive oil in a heavy-bottomed saucepan until it sizzles. Once heated, sauté the squash, shallot, parsnip, and carrot for 5 minutes or until they soften.

2. After that, sauté the bay laurel, turmeric powder, celery seeds, and fennel seeds for approximately 30 seconds or until fragrant.

3. Amaranth, soup, and water should be added. Set the temperature to simmer. For 15 to 18 minutes, simmer it with the cover on.

4. Then add the collard greens, season with black pepper and salt, and simmer for 5 minutes. Enjoy!

Nutritional Info: Calories: 196 kcal, Protein: 4.7g, Carb: 26.1g, Fat: 8.7g.

7. Chickpea, Acorn Squash, and Couscous Soup

(Preparation Time: 10 minutes | Cooking Time: 20 minutes | Serving 4 | Difficulty: Moderate)

Ingredients:

- 1 chopped shallot
- 2 cups chopped acorn squash
- 1 teaspoon garlic, finely chopped
- 1 teaspoon thyme, dried chopped
- 2 cups water
- Ground black pepper and sea salt, for taste
- 6 ounces tin of chickpeas, drained
- 2 tablespoons olive oil
- 1 carrot, chopped and trimmed
- 1 chopped stalk of celery
- 1 teaspoon rosemary, dried chopped
- 2 cups cream of onion soup
- 1 cup dry couscous
- ½ teaspoon red pepper flakes
- 2 tablespoons lemon juice, fresh

Instructions:

1. The olive should be heated over medium-high heat in a heavy-bottomed saucepan. The next step is to sauté the shallot, acorn squash, carrot, and celery for approximately 3 minutes or until the veggies soften.

2. Garlic, thyme, and rosemary are added and cooked for an additional minute until fragrant.

3. After stirring the soup, couscous, water, black pepper, salt, and red pepper flakes are brought to a boil. Turn the heat to a simmer immediately, and then cook for about 12 minutes.

4. Add the chickpeas to a can and cook for five minutes or until well heated.

5. Pour into separate bowls and top with a sprinkle of lemon juice.

Nutritional Info: Calories: 378 kcal, Protein: 10.9g, Carb: 60.1g, Fat: 11g.

8. Creamy Rutabaga Soup

(Preparation Time: 10 minutes | Cooking Time: 30 minutes | Serving 4 | Difficulty: Moderate)

Ingredients:

- 1 chopped onion

- ½ pound sweet potatoes, chopped and peeled

- ½ cup chopped parsnip

- 3 cups vegetable broth

- ¼ teaspoon dill, dried

- 1 teaspoon basil, dried

- 1 teaspoon paprika

- 1 cup water divided

- 2 tablespoons cilantro, fresh chopped

- 2 tablespoons olive oil

- ½ pound rutabaga, chopped and peeled

- ½ cup chopped carrots

- 1 teaspoon garlic-ginger paste

- Ground black pepper and salt, for taste

- ½ teaspoon oregano, dried

- 1 teaspoon parsley flakes, dried

- ½ cup raw cashews, soaked

- 1 tablespoon lemon juice

Instructions:

1. Heat your olive oil at medium-high heat in a heavy-bottomed saucepan. Then, while

stirring occasionally, sauté the rutabaga, onion, sweet potatoes, parsnip, and carrot, for approximately 5 minutes.

2. The ginger-garlic paste should be added and sautéed for a further minute or until aromatic.

3. Bring to a boil while stirring in the vegetable broth, black pepper, salt, dried dill, basil, oregano, paprika, and parsley. Instantaneously lower the heat to a boil and allow the food to cook for 20 to 22 minutes.

4. Using an immersion blender, puree the soup until it is smooth and creamy.

5. In the bowl of your food processor or blender, combine the cashews with the water, salt, and lemon juice to taste. Make a cream by blending.

6. Put the blended mixture back in the saucepan. After adding the cashew cream, simmer for five minutes or until everything is well cooked.

7. Serve using the fresh cilantro as a garnish after ladling into serving dishes.

Nutritional Info: Calories: 385 kcal, Protein: 10.3g, Carb: 33.8g, Fat: 25.2g.

9. Mexican-Style Chili Soup

(Preparation Time: 10 minutes | Cooking Time: 1 hour 5 minutes | Serving 4 | Difficulty: Easy)

Ingredients:

- 2 tablespoons olive oil
- 2 red bell peppers, chopped
- 2 chopped cloves of garlic
- 1 bay laurel
- ½ teaspoon mustard seeds
- Ground black pepper and kosher salt, for taste
- 3 heaping tablespoons cilantro, fresh chopped
- 2 cups dry red beans, drained and soaked overnight
- 1 leek, medium-sized chopped
- 1 chopped chipotle chili pepper

- 4 cups vegetable broth

- ½ teaspoon fennel seeds

- ½ teaspoon cumin seeds

- ½ cup salsa

- 2 ounces tortilla chips

Instructions:

1. Put the soaked beans inside a soup pot, fill it with new water, and cook over high heat until they boil. Boil it for 10 minutes or such.

2. After that, reduce the heat to boil and continue cooking for 45 minutes.

3. Heat your olive at medium to high heat in the same saucepan. The peppers and leeks should be sautéed for about 3 minutes or until the veggies have softened.

4. Garlic and chipotle chili pepper are added and sautéed for a further minute or until fragrant.

5. Bring to a boil after adding the vegetable broth, fennel seeds, bay leaf, mustard seeds, salt, cumin seeds, and black pepper. Lower your heat to a simmer as soon as possible and allow the food to cook for 10 minutes.

6. When everything is sufficiently cooked, stir in the saved beans and mix to simmer for another 10 minutes or so.

7. After ladling into individual bowls, serve with cilantro, salsa, and tortilla chips.

Nutritional Info: Calories: 498 kcal, Protein: 28.3g, Carb: 74.9g, Fat: 10.4g.

10. Potato Creamed Soup with Herbs

(Preparation Time: 10 minutes | Cooking Time: 30 minutes | Serving 4 | Difficulty: Easy)

Ingredients:

- 1 chopped onion

- 4 large potatoes, chopped and peeled

- 1 teaspoon basil, fresh chopped

- 1 teaspoon rosemary, freshly chopped

- 1 teaspoon allspice, ground

- Fresh ground black pepper and sea salt, for taste

- 2 tablespoons olive oil

- 1 chopped celery stalk

- 2 minced garlic cloves

- 1 teaspoon parsley, freshly chopped

- 1 bay laurel

- 4 cups vegetable stock

- 2 tablespoons chives, freshly chopped

Instructions:

1. Heat your olive oil at medium to high heat in a heavy-bottomed saucepan. Once heated, cook the potatoes, onion, and celery for approximately five minutes while stirring occasionally.

2. Garlic, parsley, basil, rosemary, allspice, and bay laurel are added and are sautéed for an additional minute until aromatic.

3. Add the salt, vegetable stock and black pepper at this point, and quickly bring to a boil. Lower the heat to boil as soon as possible and let the food cook for around 30 minutes.

4. Using an immersion blender, puree the soup until it is smooth and creamy.

5. Serve your soup hot, garnished with new chives.

Nutritional Info: Calories: 400 kcal, Protein: 13.4g, Carb: 68.7g, Fat: 9g.

11. Autumn Squash Soup

(Preparation Time: 10 minutes | Cooking Time: 25 minutes | Serving 4 | Difficulty: Easy)

Ingredients:

- 1 chopped onion
- 1 chopped bell pepper
- 4 pressed garlic cloves
- 1 tablespoon coriander, freshly chopped
- 1 teaspoon curry powder
- ½ teaspoon chili powder
- ½ teaspoon paprika
- 1 cup coconut milk, full-fat
- 2 tablespoons fresh chervil, fresh to garnish
- 2 tablespoons olive oil
- 1 large carrot, chopped and trimmed
- 2 pounds acorn squash, seeded, peeled, and cubed
- 1 teaspoon fresh ginger, minced and peeled
- 1 tablespoon Italian parsley, freshly chopped
- 1 tablespoon brown sugar
- Ground black pepper and kosher salt, for taste
- 4 cups vegetable broth
- 1 lemon, chopped into wedges

Instructions:

1. Heat your olive oil at medium to high heat in a heavy-bottomed saucepan. Now, stirring occasionally, cook the acorn squash, carrot, onion, pepper, and butter for approximately 5 minutes.

2. Garlic, coriander, ginger, and parsley are added and sautéed for a further minute until aromatic.

3. Bring to a boil while stirring the curry powder, chili powder, brown sugar, black pepper,

salt, and paprika. Instantaneously lower the heat to boil and allow the food to cook for 20 to 22 minutes.

4. Using an immersion blender, puree the soup until it is smooth and creamy.

5. Put the blended mixture back in the saucepan. After adding the coconut milk, boil the mixture for another five minutes or until it is well-heated.

6. Pour into 4 bowls and top with fresh chervil and lemon wedges to serve.

Nutritional Info: Calories: 376 kcal, Protein: 9.6g, Carb: 39.2g, Fat: 23.1g.

12. Grandma's Creamy Soup

(Preparation Time: 10 minutes | Cooking Time: 30 minutes | Serving 4 | Difficulty: Easy)

Ingredients:

- 1 chopped shallot

- 4 large potatoes, sliced and peeled

- ½ teaspoon cumin, ground

- ½ teaspoon fennel seeds

- 3 ½ cups vegetable broth

- 2 tablespoons olive oil

- 4 large carrots, sliced and trimmed

- 2 minced garlic cloves

- ½ teaspoon mustard powder

- Cayenne pepper and kosher salt, for taste

- 1 cup coconut milk

Instructions:

1. Heat your olive oil at medium to high heat in a heavy-bottomed saucepan. When the oil is heated, sauté the potatoes, carrots, and shallot for approximately 5 minutes, turning occasionally.

2. When the garlic is fragrant, add it and continue to sauté for 1 minute.

3. After stirring, add the vegetable broth, cayenne pepper, salt, mustard powder, crushed cumin, and fennel seeds, and quickly boil. Lower the heat to boil as soon as possible and let the food cook for around 30 minutes.

4. Using an immersion blender, puree the soup until it is smooth and creamy.

5. The pot with the blended soup. After adding the coconut milk, boil the mixture for another five minutes or until it is well-heated.

6. Serve heated after ladling into four bowls.

Nutritional Info: Calories: 400 kcal, Protein: 9.3g, Carb: 72.5g, Fat: 9.3g.

13. Greek-Style Tomato and Pinto Bean Soup

(Preparation Time: 10 minutes | Cooking Time: 30 minutes | Serving 4 | Difficulty: Moderate)

Ingredients:

- 1 chopped carrot

- 1 chopped red onion

- 2 minced garlic cloves

- 1 cup tin of tomatoes, crushed

- Ground black pepper and sea salt, for taste

- 1 teaspoon Greek herb mix

- 12 ounces tin of corn, drained

- 2 tablespoons parsley, freshly chopped

- 2 tablespoons olive oil

- 1 chopped parsnip

- 1 minced chili pepper

- 3 cups vegetable broth

- ½ teaspoon cumin

- 1 teaspoon cayenne pepper

- 20 ounces tin of pinto beans

- 2 tablespoons cilantro, fresh chopped

- 2 tablespoons Kalamata olives, sliced and pitted

Instructions:

1. The olive should be heated over medium-high heat in a heavy-bottomed saucepan. Now, sauté the onion, parsnip, and carrot for 3 minutes or until the veggies soften.

2. The garlic and chili pepper should be added now and sautéed for a further minute or until fragrant.

3. Bring to a boil after adding the tinned tomatoes, salt, cumin, veggie broth, black pepper, and cayenne. Lower the heat to boil as soon as possible and allow the food to cook for 10 minutes.

4. After adding the corn and beans, boil the mixture for 10 minutes to ensure that everything is properly heated. Adjust the spices based on taste.

5. Pour into individual dishes and top with olives, parsley, and cilantro.

Nutritional Info: Calories: 363 kcal, Protein: 17g, Carb: 55.2g, Fat: 10.3g.

14. Winter Root Vegetable Soup

(Preparation Time: 10 minutes | Cooking Time: 30 minutes | Serving 4 | Difficulty: Moderate)

Ingredients:

- 1 leek, large sliced

- 2 diced parsnips

- 2 diced celery stalks

- 1 teaspoon garlic-ginger paste

- ½ teaspoon caraway seeds

- 2 bay leaves

- 1 teaspoon cayenne pepper

- 4 tablespoons tahini

- 4 tablespoons avocado oil

- 2 diced carrots

- 2 cups of diced turnip

- 1 pound potatoes, sweet diced

- 1 habanero pepper, chopped and seeded

- ½ teaspoon fennel seeds

- Ground black pepper and sea salt for seasoning

- 4 cups vegetable broth

Instructions:

1. Heat the oil in a stockpot over a medium-high flame. Now, cook the leeks for approximately 5 minutes, stirring occasionally, along with the carrots, celery, turnips, parsnip, and sweet potatoes.

2. The habanero peppers and ginger-garlic paste are added, and the mixture is heated for another minute or until aromatic.

3. After that, whisk in the black pepper, salt, bay leaves, cayenne pepper, caraway seeds, and vegetable broth before bringing it to a boil. Reduce the heat to boil as soon as possible and allow it to cook for around 25 minutes.

4. Using an immersion blender, puree the soup until it is smooth and creamy.

5. Put the blended mixture back in the saucepan. After adding the tahini, simmer for five minutes or more until everything is well heated.

6. Serve hot and ladle into separate bowls.

Nutritional Info: Calories: 427 kcal, Protein: 13.7g, Carb: 41.4g, Fat: 24.2g.

15.   Golden Creamy Veggie Soup

(Preparation Time: 10 minutes | Cooking Time: 35 minutes | Serving 4 | Difficulty: Moderate)

Ingredients:

- 1 chopped yellow onion

- 2 pounds butternut squash, seeded, peeled and diced

- 1 teaspoon garlic-ginger paste

- 1 teaspoon fennel seeds

- ½ teaspoon pumpkin pie spice

- 3 cups vegetable stock

- 2 tablespoons pepitas

- 2 tablespoons avocado oil

- 2 Yukon Gold potatoes, diced and peeled

- 1 parsnip, sliced and trimmed

- 1 teaspoon turmeric powder

- ½ teaspoon chili powder

- Ground black pepper and kosher salt, for taste

- 1 cup coconut milk, full-fat

Instructions:

1. Oil should be heated over medium-high heat in a heavy-bottomed saucepan. Now, simmer the onion, butternut squash, potatoes, and parsnip for 10 minutes while occasionally tossing to achieve equal cooking.

2. The ginger-garlic paste should be added and cooked for another minute or until fragrant.

3. Before bringing it to a boil, stir in the salt, turmeric powder, black pepper, fennel seeds, pumpkin pie spice, chili powder, and vegetable stock. Lower the heat to boil as soon as possible and let the food cook for around 25 minutes.

4. Using an immersion blender, puree the soup until it is smooth and creamy.

5. Put the blended mixture back in the saucepan. After adding the coconut milk, boil the mixture for another five minutes or until it is well-heated.

6. Pour into separate bowls and top with pepitas to serve.

Nutritional Info: Calories: 550 kcal, Protein: 13.2g, Carb: 70.4g, Fat: 27.2g.

16. Cannellini Bean Soup and Kale

(Preparation Time: 10 minutes | Cooking Time: 25 minutes | Serving 5 | Difficulty: Easy)

Ingredients:

- ½ teaspoon minced ginger

- 1 chopped red onion

- 1 parsnip, chopped and trimmed

- 5 cups vegetable broth

- 2 cups kale, torn into pieces

- 1 tablespoon olive oil

- ½ teaspoon cumin seeds

- 1 carrot, chopped and trimmed

- 2 minced garlic cloves

- 12 ounces Cannellini beans, drained

- Ground black pepper and sea salt, for taste

Instructions:

1. The olive should be heated over medium-high heat in a heavy-bottomed saucepan. Now, cook the cumin and ginger for about a minute.

2. Add the onion, carrot, and parsnip at this point and continue sautéing for 3 minutes or until the veggies are just starting to soften.

3. When the garlic is fragrant, add it and mix to sauté for 1 minute.

4. Add the veggie broth after that, and then bring it to a simmer. Lower the heat to boil as soon as possible and allow the food to cook for 10 minutes.

5. After adding the kale and Cannellini beans, boil the mixture until warm. To taste, add pepper and salt to the food.

6. Serve hot and ladle into separate bowls.

Nutritional Info: Calories: 188 kcal, Protein: 11.1g, Carb: 24.5g, Fat: 4.7g.

17. Old-Fashioned Vegetable and Lentil Stew

(Preparation Time: 10 minutes | Cooking Time: 15 minutes | Serving 5 | Difficulty: Easy)

Ingredients:

- 1 onion, large chopped

- 1 diced bell pepper

- 3 cloves of garlic, minced

- 1 teaspoon cumin, ground

- 28-ounce 1 tin tomatoes, crushed

- 4 cups vegetable broth

- 1 sliced avocado

- 3 tablespoons olive oil

- 1 chopped carrot

- 1 chopped habanero pepper

- Black pepper and kosher salt, for taste

- 1 teaspoon paprika, smoked

- 2 tablespoons tomato ketchup

- ¾ pound dry red lentils, drained and soaked overnight

Instructions:

1. Heat the olive oil in a heavy-bottomed saucepan over medium heat. When heated, sauté the peppers, carrot, and onion for approximately 4 minutes.

2. The garlic should be sautéed for approximately a minute.

3. In cans, spices, ketchup, tomatoes, broth, and lentils are all added. Allow it to boil for approximately 20 minutes or until well cooked, stirring regularly.

4. Serve with avocado slices as a garnish.

Nutritional Info: Calories: 475 kcal, Protein: 23.7g, Carb: 61.4g, Fat: 17.3g.

18. Green Lentil Stew and Collard Greens

(Preparation Time: 10 minutes | Cooking Time: 20 minutes | Serving 5 | Difficulty: Moderate)

Ingredients:

- 1 chopped onion
- 1 chopped bell pepper
- 1 chopped parsnip
- 2 cloves of garlic
- 1 tablespoon Italian herb mix
- 5 cups vegetable broth
- 1 cup collard greens, torn into pieces
- 2 tablespoons olive oil
- 2 sweet potatoes, diced and peeled
- 2 chopped carrots
- 1 chopped celery
- 1 ½ cups green lentils
- 1 cup tomato sauce
- 1 cup corn, frozen

Instructions:

1. Heat your olive oil in a Dutch oven until it is sizzling. Once softened, continue to sauté the sweet potatoes, onion, bell pepper, parsnip, carrots, and celery.

2. After adding the garlic, cook for a further 30 seconds.

3. When everything is fully cooked, add the Italian herb blend, green lentils, vegetable broth, and tomato sauce. Let it simmer for approximately 20 minutes.

4. Add the collard greens and frozen corn, cover, and cook for five minutes.

Nutritional Info: Calories: 415 kcal, Protein: 18.4g, Carb: 71g, Fat: 6.6g.

19.   Cream of Carrot Soup

(Preparation Time: 10 minutes | Cooking Time: 30 minutes | Serving 4 | Difficulty: Easy)

Ingredients:

- 1 chopped onion

- 1 chopped parsnip

- ½ teaspoon curry powder

- 4 cups vegetable broth

- 2 tablespoons sesame oil

- 1 ½ pounds carrots, chopped and trimmed

- 2 minced garlic cloves

- Cayenne pepper and sea salt, for taste

- 1 cup coconut milk, full-fat

Instructions:

1. Heat the sesame oil at medium to high heat in a heavy-bottomed saucepan. Now, cook the parsnip, onion, and carrots for approximately 5 minutes, stirring occasionally.

2. When the garlic is fragrant, add it and continue to sauté for 1 minute.

3. Once the curry powder, cayenne pepper, salt, and vegetable broth have been added, quickly boil. It should cook for 18 to 20 minutes after immediately lowering the heat to a simmer.

4. Using an immersion blender, puree the soup until it is smooth and creamy.

5. Put the blended mixture back in the saucepan. After adding the coconut milk, boil the mixture for another five minutes or until it is well-heated.

6. Serve heated after ladling into four bowls.

Nutritional Info: Calories: 333 kcal, Protein: 8.5g, Carb: 26g, Fat: 23g.

20. Bean plus Vegetable Stew

(Preparation Time: 10 minutes | Cooking Time: 55 minutes | Serving 3 | Difficulty: Moderate)

Ingredients:

- 3 cups vegetable broth, roasted

- 1 chopped thyme sprig

- 3 tablespoons olive oil

- 2 chopped celery stalks

- 2 bell peppers, chopped and seeded

- 2 minced garlic cloves

- 1 teaspoon cayenne pepper

- 1 cup Anasazi beans, drained and soaked overnight

- 1 bay laurel

- 1 chopped rosemary sprig

- 1 onion, large chopped

- 2 chopped carrots

- 1 green chili pepper, chopped and seeded

- Ground black pepper and sea salt, for taste

- 1 teaspoon paprika

Instructions:

1. Bring your Anasazi beans and stock to a boil in a saucepan. After boiling, lower the temperature to a simmer. Once the herbs have been added, simmer the mixture for around 50 minutes or until soft.

2. Meanwhile, Olive oil is heated over medium-high heat in a heavy-bottomed saucepan. Now, cook the peppers, celery, onion, and carrots for approximately 4 minutes or until soft.

3. Add the garlic and cook for 30 seconds or until fragrant.

4. Cooked beans should be added to the sautéed mixture. Add paprika, cayenne, black pepper, and salt to taste.

5. For another 10 minutes, simmer, stirring occasionally, or once everything is well cooked.

Nutritional Info: Calories: 444 kcal, Protein: 20.2g, Carb: 58.2g, Fat: 15.8g.

Chapter 9: Everyday Staples: Sauces, Spreads & Salad Dressings

1. Classic Barbecue Sauce

(Preparation Time: 5 minutes | Cooking Time: 10 minutes | Serving 20 | Difficulty: Easy)

Ingredients:

- 1 cup ketchup
- 1/3 cup water
- 2 tablespoon mustard powder
- 2 teaspoons sea salt
- 1 cup brown sugar
- ¼ cup wine vinegar
- 1 tablespoon soy sauce
- 1 teaspoon black pepper

Instructions:

1. In your food processor or blender, combine all the ingredients.
2. Blend until smooth and consistent.

Nutritional Info: Calories: 36 kcal, Protein: 0.2g, Carb: 8.6g, Fat: 0.3g.

2. Walnut Ligurian Sauce

(Preparation Time: 30 minutes | Cooking Time: 0 minutes | Serving 4 | Difficulty: Easy)

Ingredients:

- 1 slice white bread, removed crusts
- ½ teaspoon garlic powder
- 1 teaspoon paprika, smoked
- 1 tablespoon basil, chopped
- Ground black pepper and sea salt, for taste

- ½ cup almond milk

- About 50 halves 1 cup raw walnuts

- 1 teaspoon onion powder

- 2 tablespoons olive oil

- 3 curry leaves

Instructions:

1. Place the bread in a dish with the almond milk and give it time to soak.

2. Add the other ingredients to the bowl of your high-speed blender or food processor after adding the soaked bread.

3. Process until it's creamy, homogeneous, and smooth.

4. Serve with zucchini noodles or spaghetti.

Nutritional Info: Calories: 263 kcal, Protein: 5.5g, Carb: 9g, Fat: 24.1g.

3. Lime, Cashew, and Dill Sauce

(Preparation Time: 25 minutes | Cooking Time: 0 minutes | Serving 8 | Difficulty: Easy)

Ingredients:

- ½ cup water

- 1 tablespoon lime juice

- 1 cup raw cashews

- 2 tablespoons dill

- Red pepper and sea salt, for taste

Instructions:

1. In the bowl of your high-speed blender or food processor, combine all the ingredients and process until everything is uniformly smooth and creamy.

2. Serve with crudités after seasoning to taste.

Nutritional Info: Calories: 24 kcal, Protein: 0.5g, Carb: 5.5g, Fat: 0g.

4. Cilantro Garlic Dressing

(Preparation Time: 10 minutes | Cooking Time: 0 minutes | Serving 6 | Difficulty: Easy)

Ingredients:

- ½ cup water
- 1 chopped red chili pepper
- 2 tablespoons lime juice, fresh
- Ground black pepper and sea salt
- ½ cup almonds
- 1 bunch cilantro
- 2 crushed cloves of garlic
- 1 teaspoon lime zest
- 5 tablespoons olive oil, extra-virgin

Instructions:

1. Blend the water and almonds and water in a blender until they are smooth and creamy.
2. Blitz the ingredients until well combined, and then add the cilantro, garlic, chili pepper, lime juice, salt, lime zest, and black pepper.
3. When everything is smooth, add the olive oil gently. Keep in the fridge for up to five days.

Nutritional Info: Calories: 181 kcal, Protein: 3g, Carb: 4.8g, Fat: 18.2g.

5. Avocado Herb Salad Dressing

(Preparation Time: 10 minutes | Cooking Time: 0 minutes | Serving 6 | Difficulty: Easy)

Ingredients:

- 4 tablespoons olive oil, extra-virgin
- 2 tablespoons minced cilantro
- 1 juiced lemon
- ½ teaspoon mustard seeds

- Cayenne pepper and kosher salt, for taste

- 1 medium-sized avocado, peeled, pitted, and mashed

- 4 tablespoons almond milk

- 2 tablespoons minced parsley

- 2 minced garlic cloves

- ½ teaspoon red pepper flakes

Instructions:

1. In a blender or food processor, combine the components above.

2. Blend until well-combined, creamy, and homogeneous.

Nutritional Info: Calories: 101 kcal, Protein: 1.2g, Carb: 4.3g, Fat: 9.4g.

6. Classic Ranch Dressing

(Preparation Time: 10 minutes | Cooking Time: 0 minutes | Serving 8 | Difficulty: Easy)

Ingredients:

- ¼ almond milk, unsweetened

- ½ teaspoon kosher salt

- 2 minced cloves garlic

- ½ teaspoon dill weed dried

- ½ teaspoon onion powder

- 1 cup vegan mayonnaise

- 1 teaspoon sherry vinegar

- ¼ teaspoon black pepper

- ½ teaspoon chives, dried

- 1 teaspoon parsley flakes, dried

- 1/3 teaspoon paprika

Instructions:

1. All the components should be properly combined in a bowl using a wire whisk.

2. Until you're ready to serve, cover and store in the refrigerator.

Nutritional Info: Calories: 191 kcal, Protein: 0.5g, Carb: 0.8g, Fat: 20.2g.

7. Homemade Guacamole

(Preparation Time: 10 minutes | Cooking Time: 0 minutes | Serving 7 | Difficulty: Easy)

Ingredients:

- 1 juiced lemon
- 1 onion, small diced
- 1 tomato, large diced
- 2 avocados, pitted, peeled
- Ground black pepper and sea salt, for taste
- 2 tablespoons cilantro, fresh chopped

Instructions:

1. In a mixing basin, mash the avocados together with the other ingredients.

2. Until you are ready to serve, store the guacamole in the refrigerator.

Nutritional Info: Calories: 107 kcal, Protein: 1.6g, Carb: 7.9g, Fat: 8.6g.

8. French Authentic Remoulade

(Preparation Time: 10 minutes | Cooking Time: 0 minutes | Serving 9 | Difficulty: Easy)

Ingredients:

- 1 tablespoon Dijon mustard
- 1 teaspoon garlic, minced
- 1 tablespoon hot sauce
- 1 tablespoon parsley, flat-leaf chopped
- 1 cup vegan mayonnaise

- 1 finely chopped scallion

- 2 tablespoons capers, coarsely chopped

- 1 tablespoon lemon juice, fresh

Instructions:

1. Mix all ingredients in your blender or food processor until well-combined.

2. Blend until well-coated and consistent.

Nutritional Info: Calories: 121 kcal, Protein: 6.2g, Carb: 1.3g, Fat: 10.4g.

9. Traditional Russian Chrain

(Preparation Time: 5 minutes | Cooking Time: 35 minutes | Serving 12 | Difficulty: Easy)

Ingredients:

- 6 ounces raw beets, peeled

- 9 ounces raw horseradish, peeled

- ½ cup apple cider vinegar

- 1 cup boiled water

- 1 tablespoon brown salt

- 1 tablespoon olive oil

Instructions:

1. Bring the water to a boil in a pot with a thick bottom. The beets should then be cooked for around 35 minutes or until tender.

2. Beets are placed in a food processor after being stripped of their skins. Blend the remaining ingredients until well blended before adding them.

Nutritional Info: Calories: 28 kcal, Protein: 0.5g, Carb: 3.8g, Fat: 1.3g.

10. Country-Style Mustard

(Preparation Time: 5 minutes | Cooking Time: 0 minutes | Serving 16 | Difficulty: Easy)

Ingredients:

- ½ cup wine vinegar

- 1 teaspoon olive oil

- 1/3 cup mustard seeds

- 1 Medjool date, pitted

- ½ teaspoon Himalayan rock salt

Instructions:

1. The mustard seeds should soak for a minimum of 12 hours.

2. Then, combine all the ingredients at a high speed until they are smooth and creamy.

3. Place in the fridge in a glass container.

Nutritional Info: Calories: 24 kcal, Protein: 0.6g, Carb: 1.7g, Fat: 1.6g.

Conclusion

A plant-based diet eliminates animal products and focuses on whole grains, minimally processed fruits, vegetables, legumes, seeds, nuts, spices, and herbs. This diet is not vegan or vegetarian; a greater portion consists of plant-based sources. Studies have shown that plant-based eating habits are beneficial, with the Mediterranean diet being the mainstay. This diet has been linked to a lower risk of metabolic syndrome, heart disease, diabetes, certain cancers, depression, and improved physical and mental health. Vegetarian diets have also reduced the risk of developing diabetes, high blood pressure, and other cardiovascular diseases.

Plant-based diets are rich in fiber, phytonutrients, protein, lipids, carbs, minerals, and vitamins required for good health. Vegans may need to add vitamin B12 supplements to ensure they get all the necessary nutrients. To change eating habits, determine why you want to do so, prepare for challenging future moments, and embrace the new phase with a positive and open perspective. Focus on the benefits of a plant-based diet and enjoy the process.

We hope you enjoyed every dish in the book. Every recipe in the book has been thoughtfully created. We sought to create straightforward dishes that are delicious and simple to prepare. The recipes also call for simple ingredients. There is no need for you to visit the food shop every day.

Made in the USA
Las Vegas, NV
14 August 2023